Emra Holmes

Tales, Poems and Masonic Papers

Emra Holmes

Tales, Poems and Masonic Papers

ISBN/EAN: 9783337074623

Printed in Europe, USA, Canada, Australia, Japan

Cover: Foto ©ninafisch / pixelio.de

More available books at **www.hansebooks.com**

TALES, POEMS,
AND
Masonic Papers,

BY

EMRA HOLMES;

WITH A BIOGRAPHICAL SKETCH OF THE AUTHOR,
BY
GEORGE MARKHAM TWEDDELL,

Fellow of the Royal Society of Northern Antiquaries, Copenhagen; Corresponding Member of the Royal Historical Society, London; Member of the Surtees Society, and of the Archæological and Architectural Society of Durham and Northumberland; Honorary Member of the Manchester Literary Club, and of the Whitby Literary and Philosophical Society; late Fellow of the Societies of Antiquaries of Scotland and of Newcastle-on-Tyne, Member of the Royal Archæological Institute of Great Britain and Ireland, the Yorkshire Archæological and Topographical Society, the Tyneside Naturalists' Field Club, the Berwickshire Naturalists' Club,
&c., &c.

NOTICE.

Any pecuniary profit that may be derived from the publication of the present volume, or of a contemplated Second Series of TALES, POEMS, AND MASONIC PAPERS, BY EMRA HOLMES, will be presented to a Brother Freemason, who has been unexpectedly plunged in poverty in the declining years of his life.

Editors of Magazines or Newspapers who may notice the present volume, whether favourably or otherwise, will much oblige by sending a copy of their Review to the Publishers.

TO

The Right Honourable Arthur Philip, Earl Stanhope,

Viscount Stanhope of Mahon and Baron Stanhope of Elvaston,

THIS LITTLE BOOK

IS DEDICATED,

AS A TOKEN OF GRATITUDE FOR MANY COURTESIES
RECEIVED AT HIS HANDS, BY

HIS LORDSHIP'S

VERY OBEDIENT SERVANT,

THE AUTHOR.

FOWEY, CORNWALL,
1877.

CONTENTS.

	Page
Biographical Sketch of the Author.	5

TALES.

The Lady Muriel	17
Gerard Montagu, a Winter's Tale	49
Ernest Blake, a Christmas Story	83
Waiting for Her, a Mesmerist's Story	106
Hopelessly; or Madge Raymond's Midnight Ride, and what came of it	136

POEMS.

Hubert and Ida, a Legend of St. Swithin's Eve	41
Autumn	81
A Thought on a Summer Sea	82
"Only a Christmas Rose"	103
A Stricken Heart	133
Old Truths	167

MASONIC PAPERS.

Notes on the old Minute Books of the British Union Lodge, No. 114, Ipswich: First Minute Book	168
Do. Second Minute Book	186
Do. Third Minute Book	200

BIOGRAPHICAL SKETCH

OF

MR. EMRA HOLMES.

During the summer of 1839, among the visitors to the pleasant village of Old Cleeve, in Somersetshire (where William de Romara founded a Cistercian monastery, in 1188, in honour of the Virgin Mary, some small portion of which yet remains, part having been turned into a private residence—where green fields, and orchards, and woodlands, supply numerous pretty pastoral pictures—and where the craggy cliffs and wild waves of the Bristol Channel, with every description of vessel bound for, or returning from, all parts of the globe, afford plentiful scope for marine views), an artist and his wife might have been observed—both, apparently, in the full flush of life—enjoying alike the pure air and the beauty of the surrounding scenery. They were a happy and a loving pair, full of high tastes and virtuous aspirations; at peace with God and all His creatures; and delighting most in each other's society. Humble as they were good and gifted (and that lady's pen was known as far, at least, as her husband's pencil), they made sunshine wherever they went; for every one felt better for having known them. Their creed might, or might not, be our creed, gentle reader; their politics might, or might not, be our party politics; but their living, practical piety was such as would recommend them to all with whom true devotion is more than their own narrow notions of theology; and their noble love of country, and strong sympathies with the poor under every possible affliction, could not but endear them to all true patriots, under whatever banner they might range themselves in the body politic. Instead of inviting rich neighbours to a wedding feast, they gave bread to the poor. Unable to carry out the now too little-heeded religious injunction of feeding the poor on the same large scale as good Bernard Gilpin, "the Apostle of the North," was accustomed to do in his hallowed manse at Houghton-le-

Spring,* in the reign of Queen Elizabeth, they did their little well every week, in their small cottage-kitchen at home, both to old people and to young children; reminding me forcibly of that fine passage in STERNE'S *Tristram Shandy* (a book, I suppose, I should be ashamed of quoting after Thackeray's cutting criticism of the author in his *English Humourists*):—"'Prithee, Trim,' quoth my father, turning round to him, 'What dost thou mean by honouring thy father and mother?'—'Allowing them, an' please your honour, three halfpence a day out of my pay, when they grow old.'—'And didst thou do that, Trim?' said Yorick. —'He did, indeed,' replied my uncle Toby.—'Then, Trim,' said Yorick, springing out of his chair, and taking the corporal by the hand, 'thou art the best commentator upon that part of the Decalogue; and I honour thee more for it, Corporal Trim, than if thou hadst had a hand in the Talmud itself."

The artist, Marcus H. Holmes, was then some thirty-six years of age; having been born at Bristol in 1803, and named after the Beresford family, one of whom, Lady Araminta Monk, was his godmother. His mother, an Irish lady, died when he was very young, and he was educated at the Bristol Grammar School, and afterwards became a student at the Royal Academy, under Fuseli, where he won the silver medal for Still Life. Returning to Bristol, he settled down there as an artist, as his father had done before him, contributing occasional pictures to the exhibitions of the Royal Academy, and to those of the Old Society of Watercolour Painters, of which both his father and himself were members; and teaching drawing in the vicinage. One of his pupils was Eugenie, the late Empress of the French, who at one time pursued her studies at Clifton. On the 12th of July, 1833, he married Miss Elizabeth Emra, one of the daughters of the Rev. John Emra, vicar of St. George's, Bristol, since which their residence had been in a pleasant little cottage, called Homefield, under the very shadow of the trees of her father's vicarage, as we shall see anon.

I have said that Marcus Holmes was also the son of an artist. His father, George Holmes, was a native of Ireland, being born at Dublin, about the year 1776; and at his father's house the ill-fated Lord Edward Fitzgerald, Theobald Wolfe Tone, the Emmetts, and other Irish patriots, who loved their country "not wisely, but too well," used to meet. He was educated at White's Grammar School, with the Duke of Wellington, Curran, Sheridan, and Tom Moore. When the chivalry of Ireland, peasant

---

* See "The Bards and Authors of Cleveland and South Durham."

and peer, formed that famous army of Volunteers, which is at
least the most gorgeous pageant that passes in view before us as
we unroll the long scroll of her sorrowful annals, and which
(could they only, Freemason-like, have elevated their mental
vision above the low and blinding mists of sectarian jealousies)
might have regenerated old Erin a century ago—George Holmes
had the honour of being one of the units which made up that
noble hundred thousand. About the year 1796, he married a
young lady from Kilkenny. It was during one of those periods
of bloodshed which have blazoned gules the vert shield of the
Emerald Isle, that a body was borne past the door of their house,
during the absence of George Holmes on duty, which his young
wife feared was that of her husband, who was uninjured; but the
shock so alarmed her that her nervous system suffered in conse-
quence, and the doctors advised her removal to England, in the
then perturbed state of the country, as absolutely necessary to
save her life. George Holmes, therefore, bade adieu to his loved
native land, and went to Bristol about 1802, where his son Mar-
cus was born in the following year. His wife dying soon after,
he removed for a few years to London, where he had published,
in 1801, a delightful octavo volume, entitled *Sketches in some of
the Southern Counties of Ireland, collected during a Tour in the
Autumn*, 1797, *in a Series of Letters*. The work is illustrated
with beautiful views of the interior of the Abbey of Holy Cross,
the cathedral-crowned Rock of Cashel, Cormac's Chapel on the
south side of the said cathedral, Ross Castle, Mucruss Lake, and
Lismore Castle, etc., from his own pencil; and the sixteen Let-
ters of which the volume is composed are not only most pleasant
reading, but are full of historical and archæological information,
both his father and himself being well versed in antiquities. The
book was dedicated to the Duchess of Devonshire, and was the
means of procuring for him the patronage of the Dukes of Lein-
ster and of Devonshire, Viscount de Vesci, and others of the
nobility.

MACAULAY has well remarked, that " it is not easy for a modern
Englishman, who can pass in a day from his club in Saint James's
Street to his shooting box among the Grampians, and who finds
in his shooting box all the comforts and luxuries of his club, to
believe that, in the time of his great-grandfather, Saint James's
Street had as little connection with the Grampians as with the
Andes. Yet so it was. In the south of our island scarcely any-
thing was known about the Celtic part of Scotland; and what was
known excited no feeling but contempt and loathing." Well then
might George Holmes write seventy-six years ago, in the Preface

to his valuable work:—"At this period of universal information, while the historic and descriptive pages of the most distant climes are unfolded to our view, are we not naturally to suppose those parts nearest the heart of the empire, through which a great portion of its life blood flows, should be intimately known? Yet, strange to say, Ireland, which, for a space of six hundred years and more, has been politically connected with, and continues to be a powerful and valuable gem, in the crown of Great Britain, is less known to the people of England, in general, than the most remote regions." It was, I believe, the first work ever published on the picturesque scenery of Ireland, and I am only sorry that my space is too limited here to favour my readers with a few extracts.

Returning to Bristol he ultimately settled there in 1808, and married a Miss Anstey, of Devizes, who bore him three children,—George, afterwards a physician, who died in Canada—Annie, married to the Rev. John Curran, a Canadian clergyman, who was great nephew of the celebrated John Philpot Curran, and cousin of the late Right Reverend Doctor Cronyn, Lord Bishop of Huron—and Mary Holmes, a lady who is still living, whose performances on the piano were very much admired at the great Exhibition of 1851, and the composer of numerous pieces of music which have been highly commended.

George Holmes claimed a "collateral descent" from Sir Robert Holmes, Charles the Second's buccaneering admiral, whom Hume terms "the cursed beginner of two Dutch wars," and to belong to a branch of the family of the Barons Holmes, of Kilmallock, in the peerage of Ireland, whose title became extinct in 1804. But as Napoleon, when offered a pedigree tracing his descent from one of the princely families of Italy, proudly exclaimed,—"Bah! I date my patent of nobility from Montenotte," the scene of his first victory as commander of an army; so may the Holmeses and the Emras safely ground their claims to the respect of their fellow-creatures on their own contributions to the civilisation of the nineteenth century, though the estates of their ancestors would be very valuable possessions.

George Holmes was the intimate friend of Bird, Danby, and Eagles (the art-critic of *Blackwood's Magazine*); was one of the leaders of the old School of Water-colour Painters; and, in conjunction with J. D. Harding, brought out lithography as applied to free-hand drawing. He died in Canada, about the year 1852, whither he had emigrated some few years before.

Such were the father and paternal grandfather of our author. Let us now briefly glance at his mother.

The Rev. John Emra, vicar of St. George's, Bristol, was the son of a West Indian slave-owner, a native of the Island of St. Christopher, and the family was supposed to be of Spanish extraction. He was sent to England to finish his education, and after leaving Oxford was ordained. He married a Somersetshire heiress, Miss Elizabeth Bastone Blake, daughter of Francis Blake, of Minehead, where two of the celebrated Admiral Blake's brothers had settled, and their descendants had continued to reside. Elizabeth Emra, one of the parson's daughters, was born, as appears by the entry in her father's Bible, November 20th, 1804. "She was," writes a sister, in a loving memoir, published in 1844,* " blessed with a considerable measure of health ; and, though her frame was small and delicate, she was not deficient in strength ; but while yet very young, she, together with several of her sisters, was attacked by the small-pox ; and, though its virulence was thought to be abated by previous vaccination, it assumed in her case a severe form, exciting painful apprehensions at the time, and long after leaving its traces on a brow and neck which had been so very smooth and fair. Her patience, however, failed not under this severe trial ; and some verses, among the first which her manuscripts contain, scarcely wanting the finished elegance of her later compositions, manifest that her fancy already roved among poetic visions, and, what is far better, that she humbled herself under the chastening of what she felt to be her *Father's* hand. They were occasioned by her being refused water, and may be thought of sufficient interest to be inserted here :—

>'Health to the sick, and cordial to the faint,
>Why is thy sparkling draught denied to me ?
>Oh ! could I see thee as thou gushest forth
>From the green hill, and murmuring glid'st along,
>Fever would leave these veins, and health again
>Bound in each pulse, and flow through every vein.
>Oh ! who will bear me to the lone retreat,
>Where freshest moss is press'd by fairy feet ;
>Where the low fern her graceful leaf extends,
>And with the wild bee's kiss the dewy primrose bends ?
>Cease, burning fever ; beating heart, be still ;
>Soul, meekly suffer ; 't is thy Saviour's will ;
>His arm sustains, his smile shall comfort thee,
>And he himself shall LIVING WATER be.'"

Not bad juvenile poetry, certainly, and giving evidence of much more brain power than was ever possessed by those miserable charlatans, whatever diplomas they may hold, the Doctor San-

---

* "A Sister's Record, or Memoir of Mrs. Marcus H. Holmes."

gradoes who delight in "thwarting nature,"—who would purge, and bleed, and blister without mercy, but could not think of allowing the parched lips of a feverish patient to be cooled with the best of all beverages for every living creature, whether in health or during disease—pure water.

From her girlhood to her grave, literature, both in prose and verse, was a source of consolation and of pleasure to her gentle spirit: for the character she depicted of good Mrs. Rachael Short, in her moral and religious tale of *Hope and Disappointment*, written only the year before her death, may be well appropriated to its gifted writer:—

"Hers was the might of exceeding gentleness; not a selfishness that sometimes gains that name, and that shrinks from personal inconvenience and exertion; but that, bearing all things, believing all things, watches its own actions and intentions with a jealous eye, and yields not one point to idleness, nor one to ease. With a frame so delicate that every exertion made it tremble, it was amazing through what hardship and trial she passed in her daily round of duty. ' *The Angel*,' the poor people used to call her; for wherever there was distress, wherever there was trouble, there came she ministering."

Miss Elizabeth Emra was a contributor of verses to *The Forget-me-Not*, one of the elegant annuals then so fashionable; and, in 1830, she published her most important work, *Scenes in our Parish, by a " Country Parson's" Daughter*; one of the best religious books I ever read, being quite free from that maudlin self-righteousness and hateful cant which too often imposes upon a credulous world for religion. Truly has TOM HOOD sung:—

> "With sweet kind natures, as in honey'd cells,
> Religion lives, and feels herself at home;
> But only on a formal visit dwells
> Where wasps, instead of bees, have form'd the comb."

You need not read many pages of either of the volumes of the *Scenes in our Parish* (for she published a second series in 1832) to be convinced that her head and heart were just what a parson's daughter's should be. "Do you love the country?" she asks, in her Introduction to the first. "Thither I will wander with you; not, indeed, through such scenery as our native land *can* show, in some of its most favoured retreats: I may gaze with you on the silver mirror of no Rydal lake; I can take you to no Walla Crag; nor, southward to the Gothic ruin, where the grass grows in the deserted aisles; and the ivy hangs in heavy wreathes round the arches, which once echoed gloriously to the Te Deum, as the music pealed from the vaulted roof, and stole over the placid

Wye: I can linger with you in no such silent and beautiful wood walks; and I may pause on no such height with you as the cliff at Piercefield: yet come with me. 'God made the country;' here are wild flowers, and clear waters, such as none but God could make: and for the stories connected with our walks;—Can you stoop to the common concerns of life? For if you enjoy nothing but romance and glowing fiction, I forewarn you that we had better part;—I never saw a knight, or a lady,—a titled lady I mean,—in my life; and the fairies of our forest forsook their haunts here, in the same day in which the first coal-pit was opened.—But have you a heart that can sympathise with human hearts, that throb, and ache, and flutter, as itself has done? Can you feel for sojourners here, who know the wear and tear of this 'work day world,' as you have known it? Will you take interest in the recital of

'Familiar matter of to-day,
  *   *   *
Some natural sorrow, grief, or pain,
Which has been, and may be again?

Above all, do you like to observe God's ways, the book of His nature and the lines of His providence? Then let us ponder over the mysterious pages together; and if we bring to the perusal simple hearts, however dim our eyes may be, I doubt not we shall study them with profit." And she tells us, in the spirit of true authorship, that she wrote " because in a life of much leisure and much retirement, it has been my greatest pleasure to do so. Hitherto, it has never been anything but an amusement, a relaxation from duties and employments, all pleasant in their way, but not one half so pleasant as this."

Living through the dreadful Bristol riots of 1831, in hourly dread of their vicarage and church being burnt by an ignorant and infuriated mob, who shouted and yelled in the name of Reform; and beholding from her father's windows and garden the raging flames which consumed the jails, episcopal palace, mansion house, custom house, and many private residences of the antiReformers; it is not wonderful that a " Parson's Daughter," who regarded the certainly ill-advised execution of Charles I, as second only in guilt to the crucifixion of Christ, should be unable to sympathise with the progress of that Constitutional Parliamentary Reform which has made our England what she is. But hear her noble tribute to the starving pitmen of her parish:— " Some of these poor fellows have walked to distant parts of the kingdom, vainly seeking employment, and come back disheartened, and weary and penniless and foot-sore. Others yet more hopelessly set out early every morning, asking for work for miles round the neighbourhood, and come back at night hungry and without means to supply their own or their children's hunger. 'I might say he's walked hundreds of miles,' said poor Patty, looking round with tears in her eyes at her husband, who sat on a low stool against the wall, gloomily leaning his head on his hands—'and now he's so weak for want of necessaries, I don't think that he could do a day's work if he had it—and indeed his shoes are quite worn out.'" And how feelingly she tells us how " when poor Joseph had known hunger and cold all through the winter, his health gave way. I have known him undertake a day's work gladly when he had not a morsel of food to take with him. He worked hard all day, from six in the morning till six at night. Twelve long hours, dear reader, in which you and I probably have had three or four meals. But Joseph worked hard all day without saying he was hungry, and it was not till his employer witnessed his eagerness to receive some broken meat offered him, in addition to his day's wages, that he had any idea that Joseph had not tasted food that day. It was no strange thing to him—but are not ours patient people? He was taken ill, and carried to the infirmary—lay ill two or three weeks, and I saw the shabby funeral procession wind its way down the road on the first Sunday in May. How sadly poor a mourning party it was you may fancy, when I tell you that it was long before the poor widow could collect eightpence to pay for turning the rusty silk of the bonnet and binding it with crape."

Though, like every other thinker, I have my own pet scheme of politics, I trust above cabal, and my own notions of theology, without wishing or believing that the Almighty Father of us all will damn those who do not see as I see; I have felt from childhood that it is not the colour of a ribbon, nor the name of a party, that makes us patriots; it is not the regular attendance at any place of worship, however good in itself, nor the mouthing of any creed, orthodox or heterodox, that makes us religious or irreligious; but whoever really serve the Eternal Spirit "in spirit and in truth," and love their neighbour as themselves, are already " accepted of God," and cannot but be useful members of any community in which their lot may be cast. Tried by this standard, the parents of Emra Holmes seem to me to have reached a much " higher level" than mankind in general, whose many money tricks are quite enough to favourably dispose one to the learned Scottish judge, poor old Lord Monboddo's theory, that they are only a civilised species of monkeys! Let us be devoutly thankful for every living argument to the contrary; and seek faithfully to so wisely fashion our own lives as to convince the world that, whatever our origin, we are not travelling monkey-ward.

It would have shown but poor appreciation of healthy English literature, if *Scenes in our Parish* had not found at least "fit audience tho' few." Among those competent judges who heartily commended it were two of our most eminent poets,—the Rev. William Lisle Bowles, then rector of Bremhill, in Wiltshire, and canon of Salisbury,—and Robert Southey, the poet-laureate; the latter of whom spoke of the "Parson's Daughter" as an honour to his and her native city; and, when paying a short visit to his friend John May, at Clifton, went and called upon her at St. George's vicarage.

"It is not needful minutely to describe the growing up of that deep affection which, blessed be God," writes her sister, "became a source of much happiness, and which succeeding years did but strengthen. He who inspired it was first known, and familiarly received, as the friend of her dear and only remaining brother. With this world's goods the young artist was but scantily furnished, but he was rich in industry and talent, in a flow of cheerful and happy spirits, and high Christian principle; and after the acquaintance of a year or two, and a few simple and prudent arrangements, Elizabeth Emra, on the 12th of July, 1833, became the wife of Marcus Holmes. It was her happy privilege to remain under the very wing of her dear and honoured parents. By an arrangement entirely in accordance with their humble and homely views, the young couple settled in a small but not inconvenient house, in what was literally 'Homefield.' * * * She greatly enjoyed her proximity to her beloved relatives, and says, in simple verse,

> 'Mine is a breezy English cot,
>   Around it many a flower
> Tells of a blest though lowly lot,
>   Of life's fresh summer hour.
>
> For Friendship there her dearest sees,
>   There kindred footsteps come,
> And the shadow of my father's trees
>   Falls on my husband's home.
>
> The same deep Sabbath bell I hear
>   As in my childhood's days,
> And the same honour'd voice and dear
>   That taught my earliest praise.'"

On the 6th of July, 1834, her first child, a girl, was born; and in 1836, she published *A Mother's Greeting to the young Members of the Church of England*, dedicated by permission to Dr. Burgess, Bishop of Salisbury. "It intends," she says, "to be an explanation of the principal seasons in our Church's year — Advent, Epiphany, &c., in as simple and affectionate language as I can write, and with a few verses of poetry to every chapter." It is a well-written commentary on the collects of the Church of England, of which she says she every day saw cause to thank God that He permitted her to be brought up a member. About the same time she commenced her *Realities of Life*, many of the articles appearing in the *British Magazine*; a second edition of the book, with three additional stories, being published in 1842, under the altered title of *Old Hetty, and other Realities of Life*.

Such were the artist, Marcus H. Holmes, and the "Parson's Daughter," his wife, with whom I opened the present paper. But why specially locate them at Old Cleeve? Let us see.

"During a week or two in the summer, the season of long days and sunny skies," writes her sister, "she was accustomed to go with her husband and a child or two, as the case might be, to an inexpensive lodging in some retired but beautiful locality, and freed in a measure from household cares, delighting in the productions of his rapid pencil, and the new and lovely scenery; she ever accounted these seasons as among the happiest in her life. * * * It was on one of these occasions that, led on by love of her pleasant holiday, and unwilling to frustrate a scheme of her kind husband's, she left home when such a step was not perhaps strictly prudent; and at the village of Cleve was born one of her little sons, in the summer of 1839. Such a delay of her return home was, of course, in many respects undesirable, and she much missed the presence and society of her dear relatives, but she was not apt to magnify an inconvenience into an affliction; the small bed-room, with its checked curtains, and the stone floor below, were no grievances to her; and full of gratitude for the conveniences ministered by the kind friends raised up around her, she wrote thus in the course of a fortnight to her anxious friends at home,—'Oh, how shall I praise the Lord for all the benefits he has shown me, forgiving all my sin, healing all my infirmities, renewing my strength like the eagle's? I certainly never had a more healthy or thriving child than my little son appears at present, and certainly never one who saw half so much company, or was so much admired. Only yesterday, two neighbouring ladies sent their footman, as I sat busy at my patchwork, to know if Mrs. Holmes was well enough to receive them? Of course I was, and, when they came, they were most anxious to know if I was the author of that BEAUTIFUL work, *Scenes in our Parish*; so I suppose the visit was rather in compliment to the book than to my son, whom nevertheless they much admired.'"

Thus the author of the following *Tales, Poems, and Masonic Papers*, was born at Cleeve, on the 4th of July, 1839. In the *Sister's Record* already quoted, we have the following description of our author's early home at St. George's:—

"We desire thankfully to acknowledge that, amid all her cares and anxieties, our dear Elizabeth had a happy and pleasant home: and oh, how kind was the greeting with which relatives and friends were welcomed there—how frank the courteous hospitality with which she produced the ready refreshment they were most likely to enjoy. A pleasant place was her sitting room: it was wonderful that so small an apartment, with so many little ones running in and out, could be always so very neat. Her books and a few drawings and historical prints, gave a finished look to the mere cottage room. For further ornament there were bright flowers fresh every day, and casts of fonts and cherub heads; there was besides a pair of antlers, festooned with various curious things, which furnished many an instructive tale to her listening children, whom she led on with happy facility from earthly to heavenly things. * * * If the day was weary, she had a smile and fond welcome ever ready for the evening, and gladly hailed the quiet hour, which, while her health lasted, she was accustomed to spend in reading to her husband, while he was busy with his pencil at her side." And if any of the children had annoyed her during the day, she did not trouble him about it, saying "it was cruel, when a man came home tired with his day's work, to be greeted with complaints of his children."

But the Rev. John Emra died, and the "Parson's Daughter" had to give up the latch key which she had hitherto had since her marriage, so as to gain admittance at will to the vicarage garden, and St. George's to her and to hers was no longer what it had been. So in December of 1842, Mr. and Mrs. Marcus H. Holmes, with their six children, removed to Westbury Hill, only a few miles off, and within easy access of her sisters' new abode. It was there that she finished and prepared for the press her last work, *Hope and Disappointment*; it was there, on the 13th of April, 1843, she wrote her last verses, "On hearing the Bells ring, on the evening of Thursday in Passion Week;" and it was there that she died in childbed, early in the morning of Tuesday, October 10th, in the same year. She herself had written, while still a maiden at home:—"It is a sad sight to see an infant in mourning for its mother, but it has been my lot to see it very often. And yet it is something more strange and sadder still, to see the bending and tottering form of the parent come, time after time, to the grave in which he longs to rest himself; but of which those whom he expected to be the strength of his age take a premature possession." And again :—" When quite young, she lost her mother; and oh, how much is told in that little sentence! How many kindnesses unperformed! sorrows unsoothed! hours of sickness unattended!"*

Mr. Marcus H. Holmes died in January, 1854, at Minehead, in Somersetshire, where he lies buried.

The Emras have been essentially a literary family; more so, indeed, than any other I remember. I could fill every page of the present volume by merely glancing at the numerous productions they have sent to the press.

A wealthy lady, in token of her admiration of *Scenes in our Parish*, hearing that the husband of the authoress was an artist not too well off in worldly matters. left a widower, with a large family, generously offered him a presentation to Christ's Hospital for his son; which was, of course, gratefully accepted; and Emra Holmes, who was just seven years of age, went to the Preparatory School at Hertford, in July, 1846. Three years afterwards, he was removed to London; and, in 1854, left the Blue Coat School, having completed his fifteenth year. He afterwards went, for two or three years, to the Grammar School at Shepton Mallett, in Somersetshire, the head master of which, Mr. John Farbrother, who was also known as the local historian of that ancient town, was a connection of the family. In March, 1857, on the nomination of R. Duncombe Shafto, Esq., M.P. for North Durham, after passing the usual civil service examination, he was appointed to a junior clerkship in the Long Room of H.M. Customs at Liverpool; and, six months later, was promoted to a like situation in the Customs at Hartlepool. There Emra Holmes remained until 1865, when he removed to Stockton-on-Tees, where he resided for two years; afterwards removing to Seaton Carew, at which little watering-place he continued to live until August 1869, when he was appointed to the first clerkship in the Customs at Ipswich. In November, 1876, he received what a recent writer in the *Civilian* calls " the blue ribbon of the civil service " by being appointed to the Collectorship of Woodbridge, in Suffolk. In April, 1877, he was removed to the more lucrative post of Collector at Fowey, in Cornwall.

Mr. Emra Holmes happening to be a resident in South Durham at the very time when I was collecting materials for biographical notices of all the poets and prose writers of the district, I could not but notice his many promising contributions to the press of

---

* " Scenes in our Parish."

the northern counties; and since then we have been for years
fellow-labourers in the London Masonic press, especially in Bro.
Kenning's excellent publications. *The Freemason,* and *The Masonic Magazine.* It was, indeed, during his residence in South
Durham that all that was manly and noble in his character first
markedly showed itself. Those public readings, which he is still
so ready to give to delighted audiences, for every good object, originated in South Durham; and there, in 1861, he first saw the
light of that glorious Freemasonry, of which he has ever since
been a teacher as well as a learner, a writer as well as a reader.
In the *Second Series,* I hope to trace his Masonic career, from his
initiation as E.A. to his highest honours, coupling therewith some
few, perhaps not altogether irrelevant, remarks on the various
degrees. Suffice it here to say, that whatever Mr. Holmes takes
in hand, he goes ahead with;—our trans-Atlantic cousins most
certainly ought to have had him, and he would have been half
way to the Presidency by this: even with us his feet fall in
pleasant places, and he succeeds where others fail. Entering the
Volunteer Artillery at Hartlepool as a simple private, in a few
years he became first lieutenant. He had scarcely smelt the salt
brine around his new home there, before he was one of the most
energetic members of the committee of the Mechanics' Institute.
As an amateur comic singer and mimic, he was so enthusiastically
successful, that he was obliged to give up both, at least as a rule,
in public company, for they interfered with his more serious
labours; but it is to be hoped that his musical voice will long be
heard in choice lectures and readings to help to elevate the tastes
of his countrymen, and his pen will long be spared to blend instruction with amusement.

On the 17th of September, 1868, Mr. Emra Holmes was united
in wedlock with Eliza, second daughter of Mr. Thomas Smith
Mawdesley, son of the Rev. Henry Mawdesley, vicar of Ramsey,
Huntingdonshire; descended from the lords of Mawdesley and
Heskin in Lancashire during at least the reigns of the first three
Henrys. By this marriage there is issue three children, Edith
Clara Mawdesley, Emra, and Marcus Henry Holmes.

Rose Cottage, Stokesley, May, 1877.

ACROSTIC

FORWARDED TO MR. AND MRS. HOLMES

ON THEIR

WEDDING DAY.

E 'en though but feebly my untutor'd muse
M ay strike the lyre, at least the lowly strain
R eceive as heartfelt and sincere, excuse
A ll imperfections nor my song disdain.

A ll that the heart can wish of happiness,
N o cloud o'ershadowing, be ever thine,
D omestic joys to comfort and to bless,

E ach pure delight that renders life divine,
L ove that can change not, friendship true to lend
I n every season its consoling ray,
Z ealous, unshrinking, faithful to the end,
A faith that passeth but with life away.

H onour, just meed of intellectual worth,
O f taste, refinement, high accomplishment,
L et all who know accord thee—'tis but truth.
M ay thus thy life in wise content be spent,
E ach passing year still bringing higher fame,
S ome fresh allurement to adorn thy name.

HARRY H. SMEYER.

Staith House,
    West Hartlepool.

THE LADY MURIEL.

CHAPTER I.

AN INTRODUCTION.

JOHN FALCONBRIDGE was an eccentric man, and one of those eccentric men whom you cannot help liking for their very eccentricity. A tall, rather plain, odd-looking fellow, with a scar on the left temple, as if from a sabre cut; carelessly, I had almost said shabbily, dressed; but with something unmistakable about his manner, which told you he was a gentleman. When we met him in Paris, at the *table d'hôte* at the Hotel de Lille et d'Albion, in the autumn of 1867, we little thought how interested we should become in *our queer bachelor friend*, as we used to call him. He used always to sit in the same place in the *salle à manger*, always wore the same dark grey shooting coat and black scarf negligently folded and pinned, the same indifferently-fitting grey trousers. He didn't seem to talk much to the people about him, as we did, but paid sufficient attention to his knife and fork to give one the idea that he was something of a *gourmet*, which was rather strengthened by observing how admirably he got served off the best dishes, and how assiduously the waiters attended to his wants, as if feeling that they at last had hit upon an Englishman who knew how to dine. My wife pitied him, because he seemed so thoroughly alone, and I determined to culti vate him, because there was an inexplicable something about the man which interested me.

When we came down on Sunday morning to go to church, our friend was in the public drawing-room, reading the *Times*. I had broken the ice the night before, by enlarging upon the weather, which, as it happened, was decidedly English and uncertain at the time; so we soon got into conversation.

"Going to church, are you?" said he. "I never go to church here; don't see the use of it. You young people do too much, see too much. St. Roche is all very well, music good, and all that; and, of course, if you haven't been there, it's as well to go, once. You should go to St. Cloud this afternoon. The fair is going on now—worth seeing for people new to Parisian life. I come to Paris for quiet, subscribe to Galignani's, spend my Sundays mostly there, take a drive in the Blois, and, perhaps, now and then pay a visit to Mabille," he added *sotto voce* to me.

"Do you know any one here?" I asked.

"In the hotel? No; haven't spoken to a soul since I came, except yourself and Mrs. ——," and here he paused, remembering that he did not yet know our names, though we had found out his from the visitors' book.

"Mildrid, dear—Mr. Falconbridge," I said, smiling, as I introduced him to my wife, at his surprise at my knowing his name. "Mr. Falconbridge—Mrs. Beverley."

We soon became great friends, and Mr. Falconbridge used to say, in his dry, quaint, sad way, "I like people to come and talk to me, and I like your wife. Come and sit near me at the *table d'hôte*, and mind I sit next your wife."

Mildrid got interested in him, and once said to me, "I am sure Mr. Falconbridge must have had some great grief, some dreadful trouble to bear. He speaks to me so gravely and sadly sometimes, and then turns it off with some sharp satirical phrase which makes me wonder whether he has a broken heart or no heart at all."

"You may be sure it's not a broken heart," I told her; "whatever women do, men don't suffer from such weaknesses."

We succeeded in getting him to go with us one day to take a drive in the Bois de Boulogne—the last day of our sojourn in the gay city. We returned just in time for *table d'hôte* at five o'clock, and rose at seven to catch the mail train at the Great Northern Line for Boulogne.

We had been laughing at some of his cynical old bachelor sayings—my wife and I—and she was wondering why, in the midst of our pleasantries, he would suddenly grow so grave.

"What was it you were telling him, Mildred, that made him laugh so much?"

"Oh, it was about my cousin Muriel's skating feat on the mere last winter, when she prevented Captain Boscawen proposing, until at last he got so tired with rushing after her on the ice that he had to give in at length, and own himself vanquished. Mr. Falconbridge asked what her name was, and when I said *Muriel* he grew pale, and seemed as if there was something painful in the name to him. Of course, I changed the subject at once. And, then, you, having sufficiently aired your French with the driver, came to the rescue."

"Ah! I fancy his is a queer history."

We were all standing in the vestibule, watching the arrivals, and waiting for a *voiture* to take us to the station, when an elderly widow lady and her daughter—apparently a lovely girl of about seventeen—arrived.

Mr. Falconbridge was scanning them in his careless manner; but as they passed us to ascend to the suite of apartments prepared for them, a troubled look came over his face, and my wife fancied she heard him say something about *Muriel* to himself, as he bid us a hasty adieu, and hurried out into the Rue St Honoré. He was going off to Baden in the morning, he remarked: might he hope to see us again; if not there, at least in England, some day?

"Come to us at Weston," I said. "We shall always have a knife and fork and a spare room at your disposal."

And so we parted, after a three weeks' pleasant acquaintance in Paris.

His address was his club, he told us the "Travellers'," and I found out afterwards that he was numbered amongst the *savans*. Blest with apparently ample means; a life of leisure; following no occupation or profession, and wandering over Europe in search of happiness, peace, and pleasure, what had that man to wish for?

Why was he so imbued with melancholy?

And who was Muriel?

CHAPTER II.

IPSWICH.—A CONFESSION.

Last summer I had a letter from John Falconbridge, in which he said he had taken a charming house in the environs of Ipswich, with pleasant grounds and a lovely view of the river Orwell. His only relative—an old aunt, Mrs. Vaux, whose husband, an army surgeon, had recently died, leaving her very poorly provided for—had come to keep the house for him, and he was preparing a home for his ward, who was coming home from school in Germany in the autumn, the climate not suiting her. The letter ended by expressing a hope that my wife and I would go and spend a month with them, as he was particularly anxious that we should make the acquaintance of the young lady.

Mrs. Beverley was unable to leave home just then, having only recently recovered from a severe illness; but I had been overworked in the office. My partner in the firm (of Beverley, Marten, and Co., exporters) had been a long business tour on the Continent, leaving me to conduct affairs at home; so my wife urged me to go, as I needed change and rest, and I was very glad to accept my friend's hospitality.

Leaving Mildrid in charge of my two fair cousins, Mary and Sophy Grey, at Weston, I took a tourist ticket for Harwich, and from thence made my way to Ipswich by one of the steamers which ply daily on the beautiful river.

It was a lovely September morning when we left the landing stage at Harwich and steamed out into the noble estuary and confluence of the Stour and Orwell—the two fine rivers joining here and flowing into the sea. As we proceeded, I was struck by the pleasing effect produced by the graceful curves in the river, with its verdant sloping banks, covered with fine trees. As one approaches Ipswich, these banks assume the dignity of hills, with handsome mansions, and a picturesque tower or church peeping out here and there from amongst the foliage. Fancy a scene like this — seagulls flying hither and thither, uttering their shrill notes; a heron stalking amongst the mud inlets in search of food; a covey of wild ducks sweeping over the water close to its surface; a yacht belonging to some noble owner at its anchorage near, with fishing craft coming in from sea; a merchantman sailing majestically by, laden with corn from the Danube; pleasure boats and fishing parties in plenty, and the bells of St. Mary le Tower ringing out a merry peal, which comes sweetly over the water; and you will not wonder that I was enchanted with these sights and sounds, the ever-varying evidences of life, joy, and beauty. We make the last bend of the river, whose serpentine course is one of its chief attractions, and as we come up get a first sight of the ancient and interesting town, lying in the hollow of a basin, its streets meandering irregularly up the gentle acclivities which pass for hills in Suffolk.

Windmills here and there crown the summits, which are covered in some parts with fine plantations; elegant villas are seen amid the trees; a crowd of churches, some of them of stately proportions, with their battlemented towers rising from the midst of the quaint gabled roofs of the old houses; and the grand Town Hall, with its lofty and beautiful clock tower, are amongst the most prominent features of the town. The elegant spire of St. Mary le Tower rises conspicuous amongst the rest. There is also a fine Custom House, with noble façade and campanile, in the Italian style of architecture, at the side of the spacious docks, and broad quays, planted with trees, and having a charming promenade, adorned with shrubs. The picture was full of interest, and could not fail to strike a stranger. The people of Ipswich are proud of their town, and show great good taste in adding to its many natural beauties.

I was delighted with my trip up the river; the distance, twelve miles, and the time occupied, only an hour and a half, being just long enough to give one pleasure without fatigue.

On landing at Stoke Bridge, I was met by Falconbridge, to whom I expressed my satisfaction at visiting so pretty a place. He expected his ward the following week. She was to come from Antwerp in one of the Great Eastern Company's boats, and we were to meet her at Harwich.

There was something odd at times about Falconbridge which almost startled me, and when I knew his history I was not more relieved.

Little by little it had come out. A chance word here, and an allusion there, piqued my curiosity, and awoke my interest. I fancied that I might do him some good if he would only confide his secret to me, and that, at all events, I could better enter into his feelings and sympathise with him; that, in short, I could be more companionable, when it seemed to me he needed a companion. I pressed him very much, therefore, to make me his confidant.

We were sitting out on the lawn after dinner, smoking our cigars, and looking at the lovely river below us, stretched out like a great lake, as it seems looking from the Belstead Road. I had been roaming about Ipswich all the morning with Falconbridge, and had drawn him out on the history of the old place, astonished to find that he was so well acquainted with the neighbourhood. He had shown me Wolsey's gate, all that remains of the college founded by the great cardinal, and I remember, on our going up Silent Street, its name struck me as being so singular.

"I thought you were, like myself, Falconbridge, until recently quite a stranger here," I remarked.

"Oh, not at all," he languidly replied; "was here ten years."

"Indeed."

"Yes. Muriel's mother was ill, and came to Dovercourt—that little watering-place near Harwich, you know—to stay, the doctors recommending the place. I took lodgings here in Silent Street, at that old house with the four gables and carved corner post. The name struck me as it struck you. Perhaps I shall go back there some day," he said gravely. "Dovercourt was a much smaller place than it is now. The lodgings were poor, and the accommodation generally bad. I don't suppose she would ever have heard of the place, which has wonderfully improved of late, but that her husband had the remnant of a once large property in the neighbourhood, and the second title in the family was Lord Chelmoudiston. However, the sea air was too keen, and she did not get any better, so I took a small house for her here on the Woodbridge Road, about a mile and a half from the centre of the town. They have built quite a little colony there now, and call it California; and there she lived with a maiden aunt of hers, Miss Lacy, and little Lady Muriel."

"These strawberries are very fine ones, Falconbridge."

"Well, yes; they are grown here."

"What a fine view that is, to be sure! This is a charming place. By the way, the lady you spoke of this morning was a relative of yours, I suppose."

"Oh, not at all. She was a widow, with aristocratic connections, but very few friends in the world, and I was, I fancy, the best able to be of use to her."

"You interest me much. Pray who was she?"

"Well, when I first knew her she was Muriel Aldithley, a governess in the family of one of the canons at Canchester.

The Aldithleys were poor, but they came of a good stock. I have a daguerreotype on the mantelpiece in the dining-room—you noticed it perhaps—by Claudet."

"I did; a fair lady, with light brown hair and very large blue eyes, something like the young lady who came into the hotel at Paris last year just as we were leaving, you remember."

"Yes, you are right; there was a likeness. Well, that was Muriel's mother."

"She must have been a lovely woman. Was she an old friend of yours?"

"Hum—rather. I knew her, I suppose, ten years."

"Intimately?"

"Intimately."

"Pardon my curiosity," I said, "but it seems so strange to me—a middle-aged bachelor becoming the guardian of a young lady whose mother (a lady of title, as I conclude) was no connection, only the friend of a man who, of all others, seems to me the least likely to be impressed by female charms or to be affected by female weaknesses, and who, I should think, could hardly plead guilty to a Platonic attachment."

"Hum. My dear fellow, perhaps I'm more romantic than I look. You are a married man, and a deuced lucky fellow. However, I am not. I thought I should be once, though."

"Why don't you marry, man? You've lots of property; you are not old—five-and-forty must be the outside of your age; and lots of nice girls would have you."

"Very possible, I dare say; but there was but one woman whom I cared for."

"What was her name, if I may ask?"

"Muriel Aldithley."

CHAPTER III.

JOHN FALCONBRIDGE'S STORY.—MURIEL ALDITHLEY.

"It was in the winter of 1850," Falconbridge said, "that I first met Muriel. She was then governess at Canon Pennyfather's, at Canchester, as I think I told you. I was then a lieutenant in a line regiment stationed there. The county ball was given on the 20th of December, and the officers of my regiment were invited. One of them, Auberon Mandeville, the captain of my company, a dissolute fellow, but a man very highly connected, was one of our number who went. Muriel was there with the Miss Pennyfathers, and was at once singled out for a great deal of attention, on account of her graceful manners and beautiful face. I've seen many lovely women since, but never one to equal her. I danced a great deal with her; so did Mandeville; and the fellows at mess next day chaffed us about our making such a dead set at *la belle* Aldithley. I was younger then than I am now, and some light words that Mandeville dropped about her nettled me; we quarrelled; and duelling being out of fashion, we satisfied ourselves, I suppose, with a mutual 'cut.' About a month after the ball, I had been spending the evening with a fellow called Bloxam, who had taken me several times to the Pennyfathers, who were connections of his, and we had all become great friends. Muriel had become to me something dearer than a friend—but more of this anon. Well, Bloxam and I were strolling home rather late (twelve o'clock, I expect) to my quarters. We had to pass through the Close to take advantage of the short cut. My friend, being a nephew of the Dean, could always get through the great gates, which were closed at eight o'clock, when the curfew rang. Just as we past the Deanery, we heard voices talking close to the carriage entrance to the Pennyfathers. I thought I recognised one of the voices, but was not sure. Curiosity, or perhaps some deeper feeling, drew me to the spot, and then I found that the men, whoever they were, had got somehow into the garden, and it was clear that one of them at least was the worse for liquor. From what I could gather, it seemed that the fellow who was tipsy was asking the other two to assist him to carry off Miss Aldithley, and I soon found out by the voice that it was no other than Captain Mandeville who was speaking, his Irish experiences evidently telling upon him in his present state; for I cannot believe that in his sober senses the fellow would have thought for a moment on anything so mad as this scheme. The other two men were to go—the one to the front, the other to the back of the house. The young lady was quite agreeable it seemed—so Mandeville said ; and the concerted signal was a low whistle given three times. When this was heard, the man at the front of the house was to hurry off to the Elms (the name of one of the Canons houses in the Precincts), where a cab was standing waiting to take home some of the company from a dinner-party. The cabman had been bribed with a sovereign to come at once. Mandeville and the young lady, who would get out of the bedroom window, and come down by a ladder the other man had procured and placed against the wall, would go off in a cab, as if from the dinner. Dr. Pennyfather was away, and only the two daughters, the governess, and two maid servants were in the house. It was clear to us that the men were making a tool of Mandeville, and that they intended to commit a burglary.

"I had my reasons for believing that Miss Aldithley, so far from meditating an elopement with Mandeville, rather favoured my pretensions, and it must be owned I was desperately in love with her.

"Judge, then, of my amazement and indignation, when I overheard this dastardly scheme for kidnapping the girl I loved best in all the world. There was not time for anything but immediate action. I knew that my brother in arms was of so *noble* a nature that he would not scruple about ways and means to effect his purpose; and I knew also that Muriel did not comprehend that the handsome " officer " was nothing more nor less than a thorough scamp. The wall was too high to climb, but they must have entered by the back gateway, which had probably been left unfastened. Bloxam went round to the back at once to let loose the great St. Bernard dog, which knew him, whilst I went to the front to intercept the man who had gone for the cab. The preconcerted signal was heard just as I got to the garden gate, and a man passed me running stealthily under the shadow of the wall. The rattle of a cab and a shrill scream sounded on my ear. Making my way round to the side of the house, I saw Mandeville at the top of the ladder, and the white form of a woman apparently leaning out of the window. A sudden crash, and the ladder had fallen down with its burden. A hoarse bark, and up bounded " Lion " to my assistance as I was struggling with one of the fellows, who I found had been trying to get into the kitchen window, and whom I had collared. Presently a policeman came upon the scene; and, as I had stunned one of the fellows, and the dog had pinned the other, we soon managed to give them into custody. Mandeville's arm was broken, and we had to assist him into the cab—which was made a very different use of to what was intended—and he was taken home. The papers got hold of a queer version of the affair. I afterwards learned that Miss Aldithley had formed an attachment to Captain Mandeville, which I did not credit; but for her sake, and for her character, I was silent about the matter. The *Hampshire Gazette* stated that 'a daring attempt at burglary had been made at the house of one of the Canons residentiary of Canchester, and but for the prompt arrival of two of the officers of the 57th Regiment, and the heroic conduct of Captain Mandeville—who, seeing one of the robbers enter through the window of one of the rooms, followed the man, and, after a desperate struggle, succeeded in saving the property, and probably the lives, of some of the inmates, though it regretted to say he had sustained considerable injury, and had his arm broken in the attempt—the consequences might have been serious.' Bloxam and I held our peace, and the story told, no doubt. If I had ever said anything to Miss Aldithley which could be construed into a disparaging remark about Mandeville, Muriel put it down to my jealousy; and though I continued to pay her devoted attention, she seemed to be changing towards me. The truth must be told, I began to hate Mandeville; yet it must be owned he was a fascinating fellow where he chose to fascinate.

"Muriel soon grew to like—and, I fancied, to more than like—him. He was always putting himself in her way, and there were few women who could resist him. Only a few days before the burglary, I had proposed to, and, as I thought, had not been rejected by, her. She had not then come under his baneful influence. I felt, therefore, that I was justified in speaking to her about him; but she was, it must be owned, a flirt. To my astonishment, when, some day's afterwards, Captain Mandeville's name came up in the course of conversation, Muriel said,—

"'It is quite clear, Mr. Falconbridge, that you are jealous of Captain Mandeville, and you cannot trust me. We had better, therefore, part.'

"'Muriel,' I answered, 'you misunderstand me. I bear him no ill will, and you ought to know how devoted I am to you; pray unsay what you have just said.'

"'I do not wish to quarrel with you,' she answered, 'but I am tired of this espionage. I intend to be free again, and so good morning, Mr. Falconbridge,' and with that she sailed out of the room.

"I could not believe it; it seemed all like a dream; and it was some time before I could realise the fact that I was a *discarded lover*. The next day I called again. She would not see me. I wrote, asking for an explanation. My letter was returned, and a pretty little emerald ring I had given her was sent back. I was dreadfully cut up about it; but, then, you see, I was 27, and she 20. I buoyed myself up with the hope that she was infatuated with this man; that the thing would wear off; and that, in time, it would all come right again. Our regiment was ordered to Chatham, and I never saw or heard anything more of Muriel for three years. I wrote to her once a year during that time, telling her that whenever she chose to change her mind I was ready and willing to keep my promise if she would only keep hers. The first time she returned my letter without comment; the second year she wrote me a civil little note, saying she was engaged to Captain Mandeville. He had exchanged into another regiment, and was going out to India. When last I heard—it was soon after I had written to her for the third time (I always wrote on the anniversary of the day I first met her at the county ball)— in reply she sent me this;" and, as he spoke, Falconbridge pulled out of his vest a small Russia leather pocket-book, and taking out one little perfumed sheet of paper, read the following:—

"'Dear Mr. Falconbridge,

"'I am going to be married to-morrow, and I want you to forgive me the wrong I did you three years ago. I fear I did not know my own mind then; perhaps I do not know it now. I shall always look upon you as a dear friend, and I feel that I was quite unworthy of your love. Will you forgive me?—Your sincere friend,

"'MURIEL ALDITHLEY.'

"The next day I saw the announcement of her marriage to Major Mandeville."

"How did you answer that letter? It sounds like the letter of a kind-hearted woman?"

"Well, I kept a copy of my answer, because I thought that the sentiments I then expressed I might, by constant reiteration, teach myself to feel, and I used to take out the letter and read first hers and then my reply. You can read it if you like."

I took the paper from him, and read as follows:—

"MY DEAR MISS ALDITHLEY,—

"Thank you very much for your kind letter. I shall prize it dearly, as I prize anything of yours. I forgave you long ago, and now that you are married, I shall do my utmost to forgive your husband. He knew I loved you, and knew also that you were affianced to me. He came between us, and I can hardly blame you for admiring one who was so much handsomer and richer than I.

"It is I who ought to beg you to forgive me for aspiring to your hand. Our paths are different now. You go to India; our regiment is ordered to Canada; we may never meet again. Pray remember this, however, that if ever I can render you a service, if ever I can be of any use to you, command me, and I will as happily obey your wishes as if I had not been,—Your discarded lover,

"JOHN FALCONBRIDGE."

CHAPTER IV.

LADY MURIEL.

"What became of the lady?" I asked.

Falconbridge was in a profound reverie, and took no notice. At last, with a sort of half-start, he seemed to recover himself, and said,—

"Pardon me, my thoughts were far away. Did you speak?"

I repeated the question.

"Oh, ah, yes; I will tell you. It was only six months after her marriage that, by the sudden death of Mandeville's cousin, whose only son had predeceased him by a few months only, he came into the earldom of Kilpatrick, and my friend became an Irish Countess. He did not enjoy the dignity long, however, for, four months afterwards, I saw his death in the papers, which occurred through a fall from his horse in the hunting-field, and at twenty-four Muriel was a widowed Countess, and would shortly become a mother. In the event of there being no son, the title and estates went to a distant cousin, and the Earl, always a careless man and by no means a loving husband, had made no provision for his widow whatever. Poor thing! it was a time of great anxiety for her. If, in the course of the next three months, she should happily become the mother of a boy, he would be the eighth Earl of Kilpatrick, the possessor of a proud title and ample estate, and she, as his mother and guardian, would live in comfort and even affluence. If, on the contrary, the posthumous child should be a girl, she would be left almost penniless and without a home. The family had never taken any notice of her, always talking, as I heard, of "that dreadful *mésalliance*," as they were pleased to call it, with much disdain. It was not likely, therefore, that she would look to them for anything. Meanwhile, of course, she was left in possession at Castle Court. I did not go to Canada after all. Our regiment had been ordered out to the Crimea, the war having broken out. I should have preferred staying in England for her sake, especially just then; but no man of honour could leave the army at such a time. I suppose it was owing to her trouble and anxiety, poor thing! but the little stranger made its appearance two months before it was expected, and it was a girl. The news reached me just two days before I sailed, and I went immediately to my bankers, arranged for the purchase of £10,000 worth of consols—almost the whole of my available property then—and had it entered in her name, so that she should not be entirely penniless. I left instructions also that £200 should be immediately paid her, and that the money should be conveyed in such a manner as to lead her to suppose it was her husband's property. I well knew that her proud spirit would not allow her to receive it from me. The next news I heard was that she had left Castle Court with her child, and had gone to Ryde for the winter. I did not meet her for three years, though I had taken occasion to write to her once or twice to proffer my services if she needed them, and she always wrote me pretty frank replies.

"It was in the spring of 1857 that we met, soon after my return from the Crimea. Directly the war was over I sold out, making up my mind to ask her to marry me. From motives of delicacy I had refrained from approaching her as a lover hitherto, because I knew she felt her husband's death very much, though he had not treated her kindly. As I told you, however, she was ailing, and in 1858 I took lodgings for her at Dovercourt, the doctors recommending her to leave Derbyshire, where she then was, and try the sea air for herself and the little girl. I grew very much attached to the little Muriel, as you may imagine, for she was very like her mother ; and her delicacy of health, whilst it endeared her more to her mother, perhaps, was not the less attractive to me. Poor girl! I could not bear to lose her now ; it would break my heart. Well, Lady Kilpatrick at length grew, I think, to like me enough to promise me her hand, and we were to be married in the autumn of that year. But, to my great grief, as the summer drew on, she had another attack of the disorder with which she had been previously afflicted. It baffled the skill of the doctors, and soon her days were numbered, and I found that I must lose the only friend, the only woman whom I loved in the world. A countess is never without friends of a sort; but Muriel was not rich enough to mix in the society her rank would warrant, and the circumstances of her life, the troubles she had passed through, and her always delicate health, combined to make her lead a very *secluded*—ill-natured people called it a very *exclusive*—life. She was an interesting invalid— a lady of title, whom every one knew by name and by sight; but no one intimately ; and although many people of position called upon her at Ipswich, she always returned their calls, and the acquaintance ended there. Not that she was proud—far from it ; but the circumstances of her life altogether, as I have said, led her to live secluded and much alone.

"It was just such a day as this, I remember, that I saw her last—a lovely, soft autumn day. She was much better, and had so far recovered that she could be carried into the garden to enjoy the balmy air and the beautiful sunlight.

"'John,' she said, 'I feel better to-day, much better. If I recover, I will try to be a good wife to you.'

"'God grant you may, dear,' I answered.

"'But if I should not, you will be good to Muriel, will you not ?'

"'She shall be as dear to me as if she were my own child.'

"'Thank you! you are too good to me and mine,' she answered, with the tears welling up into her beautiful eyes.

"Beverley, you don't know what I have gone through.

"The doctors buoyed me up with hopes that she would recover. Mrs. Vaux thought that she was gaining strength daily. So much better was she that I took a house, and had already commenced furnishing it in anticipation of a coming event which was to bring such happiness to me, when one morning I was hastily summoned to Kilmallock Lodge, only just in time to find that Muriel had broken a blood-vessel, and was rapidly sinking. In an hour from my arrival, she was no more!

"Man, I cried like a child! the blow was almost too heavy to bear. The one hope, the life, the joy of my heart was gone, and only coldness and weariness remained.

"I have smiled sometimes to find, by some chance expression of yours, that you fancied me a gloomy misanthrope, a cynic, a misogynist.

"I suppose you little know how much I have gone through. Well, to make a long story short, I may tell you that the noble relations who had held aloof from her whilst alive, now she was dead, took her from me, and laid her in the burial ground at Castle Court beside her husband. The grand funeral—what a mockery it was to treat her as a countess only when she was dead! The thing disgusted me. They offered to take the little girl to educate; but Muriel's last request was that I should take care of the child, and I would not give her up to them.

"After Lady Kilpatrick's death I couldn't stay in England.

"I got unsettled, and roamed about, visiting, in the course of my rambles, Baden, Paris, Biarritz, Vienna, Rome, Switzerland, but could not bear to abide in any place long at once, and thus spent some years seeking for relief in change of scene and company.

"I don't suppose I have led a very good or useful life. On the contrary, I have wasted my time a good deal, I dare say; and, to tell you frankly, I think it was through meeting you last year in Paris that I was led first to think of coming back to England and settling down. Muriel's health, too, not being very good at Heidelberg, where I sent her as soon as she was old enough to leave England, made me resolve to make a home for her here.

"I had spent a fortune abroad; but some capital investments here have more than recouped all I lost there.

"Of course, my ward gets all I have when I die."

"Do you believe in these capital investments?" I asked.

"Oh, yes, I'm secure enough. Half my property is invested in the great shipbuilding company in the north—Waters, Waters, and Company."

"The deuce it is," I said.

"Yes; and it will be a fine property for Muriel some day, man! you see if it isn't.

"Poor child! she is now fourteen; how the time goes! I am going to have a resident governess here for her, besides teachers from the town; and I particularly wanted Mrs. Beverley to be here just now to give me advice about her."

I had listened attentively to Falconbridge's story, and could not help pitying him as he told it.

Two or three days afterwards he came down very much excited, and told me he had received a letter from the people at Heidelberg with whom Lady Muriel resided, and was sorry to find that she had been ill; but the letter said she was now better, and would come by the boat the next day (Thursday).

We decided to take *circuit* tickets, and go down by the boat, returning by the train with Muriel. On our way down, I noticed something very strange in Falconbridge's manner, which startled me. He complained of his head, which reminded me that he had received a sword-cut on his forehead in the Crimean war, which had affected the brain at the time, but from which he had long recovered, as I thought.

He was talking rather gloomily, and said something about Muriel; if anything should happen, I should find his will all right.

I rallied him about being so dispirited, but without much effect.

When we got to Harwich, we found that the boat had not come in from Antwerp, but a telegram awaited Mr. Falconbridge. It was dated from the Hotel de l'Europe, and it informed him in the usual curt way that "Lady Muriel Mandeville was unable to proceed. It was feared she was dying."

I shall never forget the ashy paleness that overspread his face when he read the intelligence.

I tried to rouse him, but without effect for some time. He sat down in the hotel that we had gone to, read the telegram, and the tears coursed down his cheeks as he said to himself,

"Poor child! poor child!"

It was a pitiful sight to see a man like him, usually so difficult to move, completely broken down.

Shall it be owned, my own eyes moistened as I heard him saying over those words to himself, like one dazed,

"Poor child! poor child!"

The next boat did not leave for Antwerp till the following evening, and I persuaded him to come back with me to Ipswich. For some reason or other he would go back by boat, instead of taking the train.

CHAPTER V.

VERY NEAR TO SILENT STREET.

"The day is lovely," I said, trying to get him to talk to me as we made our way down to the steamboat.

"Yes."

"Aren't you well, old fellow?"

"Oh, yes. I'm all right," he answered, looking straightforward at vacancy, and seeming to see nothing.

"Take a glass of brandy before we go," I urged. "You look pale, man, and knocked up."

"No, thanks, I'm all right."

We had brought down his St. Bernard dog, Lion, with us. The poor beast often came with us in our walks, and having followed us to the station in the morning, we had allowed him to accompany us. At Harwich we missed him, however; but just as the steamer started, it tracked us out, and, coming down with a bound on the landing stage, at once leapt into the water and swam after us. It was a faithful beast; a shaggy, fawn-coloured coat, and a large, beautiful head, with great foolish, loving eyes, as mild as any woman's, and a temper as placid and good as ever dog owned.

Falconbridge was very fond of it, for it was a present from Lady Kilpatrick, to whom it had been given by the Misses Pennyfathers, and its sire was the same dog that figured in the memorable scene years ago at Canchester.

The poor thing barked and swam after us as fast it could, but the steamer soon got ahead, and I feared the dog would be drowned. On any other occasion Falconbridge would have been the first to go to the rescue of poor Lion; but there he sat moodily with his face buried in his hands, taking no heed of what was passing by. At last I went to the captain, who good-naturedly stopped the boat, and in a few minutes we got the faithful beast on board.

It immediately ran to its master, and crouched at his feet, but he took no notice of it.

I was walking to the other end of the vessel, when there was a sudden cry,

"A man overboard!"

A rush to the side of the vessel, which was immediately stopped, showed me Falconbridge in the water. A loud bark and a great plunge, and "Lion" was seen swimming with his arm in its mouth.

To lower the boat, to take up the body, was the work of a minute or two only; to restore consciousness took a much longer time.

I hurried down into the cabin, which was cleared of passengers, and there was the dog whining pitifully, and licking his master's hands, which hung down lifelessly by his side.

But, thank God! he was saved, though it was long before he recovered. When he did he was a changed man.

* * * * *

It appeared that some one had lent him the day's newspaper; he took it, out of civility, for a moment, and as he handed it back with thanks, his eye caught the heading of a paragraph:— "Failure of the great Shipping Company—Waters, Waters, and Co." The sudden shock caused by seeing this news of the wreck of his fortunes was too much for him. A sudden, dreadful impulse seized him, and he sprang over the side of the vessel, intending to end his troubles there and then. He recovered, however, and so did Lady Muriel.

Waters, Waters, and Co., only suspended payment for a time, and now are as prosperous as ever.

Ipswich and its associations were too painful to poor Falconbridge, and he soon gave up his house there, and he and his ward and Mrs. Vaux have come to reside near us at Weston.

Little Lady Muriel promises to be as beautiful and accomplished as her mother, and she loves John Falconbridge quite as much as if he had been her father.

The last time I saw him he had but lately become convalescent. He said,

"Well, old fellow, I was very near *Silent Street*, wasn't I, that day? I was out of my mind then, I have fancied since, and if it had not been for 'Lion,' Lady Kilpatrick's last present to me, my dear little Muriel would have been left without a protector; but God has been very good to me, and I trust I may never forget His many mercies."

HUBERT AND IDA.

A LEGEND OF ST. SWITHIN'S EVE.

Glorious sunset rays were glinting,
   Hill and dale, and mount and lea;
Purpling white smoke curling upwards
   From the minute gun at sea.

Tinting all the rippling waters,
   And the vessels sailing o'er;
Making golden tower and steeple,
   With the glories as of yore.

Twilight came upon the ocean,
   Came and touch'd the ancient town;
Slumb'rous shadows brooded over
   Lofty headland, noble down.

And the curfew, sounding sweetly,
   Caught by western evening breeze,
Floated over town and steeple,
   Over those soft summer seas.

All around seem'd calm and peaceful,
   All on earth, on sea, and sky,
Just as if there were no sorrow,
   Strife, or discord ever nigh.

So thought Countess Eva gravely,
   As she look'd o'er sea and land;

Look'd out westward through the gloaming,
    Seeking loved ones on the strand.

One, a fair and stately maiden,
    Eldest of a noble band,
And another loved as fondly,
    Walking with her hand in hand.

Sauntering careless in the twilight,
    Over shingle, yellow sand,
In and out, o'er rocks and caverns,
    Still they linger hand in hand.

Now the tide is creeping, crawling,
    Like a treacherous snake it moves,
Slowly round the cliffs and upwards,
    Towards those Countess Eva loves.

Looking down from beetling crag-path,
    High above the fated pair,
Countess Eva sees the peril
    Of the dear ones loitering there.

The summer morn a path of glory
    Spreads across the glassy sea;
Billow over billow rolling,
    With a soft sound ceaselessly.

Onwards with a stealthy motion,
    Like a truant creeping home,
See the tide comes sweeping, flowing,
    With the white crest of its foam.

In the pathway of the moonbeams,
    Where they shimmer on the strand,
By chill waters now surrounded,
    Still they wander hand in hand.

Seeking here and there some outlet,
    Hoping yet some path to find,

Which may lead them yet to safety.
    Leaving treach'rous sands behind.

Vainly do they call for succour,
    None are near to help and save ;
Rushing waters come between them,—
    Both must find a watery grave.

Oh ! the terrible despairing,
    Oh ! the anxious, bitter cry
Of the mother who, above them,
    Standing breathless, sees them die.

Sees the waters lapping round them,
    Narrowing ever where they stand,
Till a last, sad vestige only
    Now remains of shifting sand.

And the lover's mute appealing
    To the God who reigns above,
Seems but mock'd by swelling waters,
    As they bear him from his love.

So in death e'en they're divided,
    For a cruel hungry wave
Carries her away, and sunders
    That brief union in the grave.

A love of years, a love of childhood,
    Which had only grown with time,
Now to close, oh, bitter ending !
    Just when both are in their prime.

Still he would have borne it bravely,
    Call'd that bitter past but sweet,
If the false sea had not robb'd him,
    E'en in death of her so sweet.

Parted by the glittering wavelets,
    Flashing idly on the shore,

Just a little distance only.
    But to meet, oh! nevermore.

From the grave he could not save her,
    Though he now himself might save,
For a huge wave bears him safely
    To the shore, to find—a grave.

Just across the streak of glory,
    Comes a shadow and a cloud;
Winds are rising now and sobbing
    As of death, and of a shroud.

Dimly sees he coming towards him,
    Washing nearer with each wave,
What was only now the maiden
    Whom he loved, but could not save.

Clamb'ring up on rock above him,
    Looking down on that sweet face,
Borne so close beneath him, peaceful,
    Full till now of light and grace!

Can he live now she is taken
    From his side in fear and pain?
Can he look on her fond mother?
    Ne'er on this earth, ne'er again.

She, the stately, noble lady,
    Standing awestruck, shrieks for aid;
But, alas! no echo answers;
    All her last hopes sadly fade.

Grief and fear o'ercome the mother,
    Standing 'neath that placid moon;
Calling vainly for assistance,
    Sinking down in helpless swoon.

But the lover hears the last cry,
    Dimly distant though it seems;

Just as one hears sounds and voices
　　In the visions that are dreams.

Dimly sounds the shrill beseeching
　　Wail that comes along the breeze:
Like the cry of some strange night-bird,
　　Heard 'midst grand old forest trees.

Something told him that a mother's
　　Sad lament gone up on high,
Had repeated the old story—
　　Earthly love is born to die.

That this world is not for ever;
　　That here pleasure turns to pain;
And the happiness of summer
　　Soon brings winter in its train.

And with one wild sob of madness,
　　Holding life without her cheap,
Looking down upon the waters,
　　Hubert took the fatal leap.

Down where Ida fair was lying,
　　In a little fairy cove,
Where the straggling moonbeams wander'd,
　　And the wave plash'd soft above.

*　　*　　*　　*　　*

And the fishers tell the story,
　　How one, passing on the cliff,
Saw the tragedy enacted,
　　Saw the corpses stark and stiff.

When the tide had slowly fallen,
　　Leaving these two on the shore,
He descended, with another,
　　And with help the lovers bore

Up the craggy path, and homeward
    To the castle of the lord,
Where the sad tale they related
    Of the daughter he adored.

Side by side the lovers lie now,
    In the great ancestral tomb,
'Neath the stately fane, where slumber
    All the dead in endless gloom.

Countess Eva now amongst them:
    Never did she come again,
But on that drear night she wander'd
    Over breezy down and plain;

Gone distraught, and always asking
    When would Ida e'er return?
Sinking slowly, ever sinking,
    Her life's lamp doth feebly burn.

And at last the Countess Bertram
    Went the way we all must go;
And the old baronial mansion
    Was once more the house of woe.

Now they all are gone and vanish'd;
    Naught remains to tell of those,
Save the sculptured urn and hatchments,
    Showing where they now repose.

But the fishermen still show you
    That great rock, the Lover's Leap,
And the Fairy Cove, and tell you
    Tales that make your cold blood creep.

How once every year at even
    Two young forms do wend their way,
Over sand and over shingle,
    Towards the cliffs near the bay.

How the tragic scene's repeated
    Where the faithful lovers died,
Where the bodies were discover'd,
    And the mother wildly cried.

And some think the place is haunted,
    But of that I cannot say;
Only on St. Swithin's even,
    Naught would make me pass that way.

   *   *   *   *   *

Still the glorious rays are glinting
    Hill and dale, and mound and lea;
Still the white smoke purples upwards
    From the minute gun at sea.

Just another cloudless even,
    Like the time I said before;
And the sunset on the steeple
    Brings back glories as of yore.

Tell such stories as I tell now,
    Of a day now long gone by;
Just to bring back the remembrance
    Of some lost chord silently.

Some sweet scent—a sound of music—
    Some one word—how oft they bring
A joy, a sorrow, or a something
    That perchance to which we cling.

So this hour and day have brought me
    Back to this old legend too;
And I tell you as I've heard it,
    Vouching that at least 'tis true.

And if you can find that old town,
    Which stands nobly by the sea;

With its church, an ancient building,
　　Founded by the Bruce, say we:

Men, on asking, they will show you
　　Fairy Cove and Lover's Leap;
And I trow will show you also
　　Those grey cliffs so bold and steep.

GERARD MONTAGU:

A WINTER'S TALE.

SEQUEL TO THE "LADY MURIEL."

CHAPTER I.

ALL HALLOW EVE.

It was All Hallow Eve, the year of grace one thousand eight hundred and sixty-nine, and a pleasant party were sitting round a table in the drawing room of one of the new villas just built at the outskirts of Weston-super-Mare. The evening was cold, and a good fire burned in the grate, the warm curtains were drawn, and there was a cosy winter-evening aspect about Chantry Villa pleasant to contemplate.

My dear old bachelor friend, John Falconbridge, and his ward had come in to spend the evening with us, and we were keeping Lady Muriel's birthday.

Lady Muriel Mandeville was John Falconbridge's ward. There was no relationship between them, but we had heard (indeed he told me himself) a sad story about his being engaged to her mother, the young Dowager Countess Kilpatrick, and how she died, and he adopted her daughter, then a little girl.

John wanted us very much to spend the evening with them—their house was close to ours—but Mildred had asked Gerard Montagu to tea with us that evening, and so they all came in to spend Halloween with us.

Old Mrs. Vaux, Captain Falconbridge's aunt and housekeeper, was unwell, and begged to be excused, but we were a pleasant little party nevertheless.

My wife came into the room saying, "Fred, what do you think those silly people are doing in the kitchen? Margaret and Ellen are burning nuts on the fire place, and Margaret is almost crying with vexation because she and John won't burn together."

"What does it all mean, Mrs. Beverley?" Lady Muriel asks.

"Why, don't you know that on Halloween people burn nuts together on the hob? You take two—one is yourself, and the other is your lover. Well, if they burn slowly together, side by side, then you will be married; if a nut cracks or jumps, your lover will prove unfaithful. It is an Irish custom, I believe."

"And a Scotch one, too, my dear," I said, correcting Mildred, "don't you know Burns' poem, *Halloween?*

> 'The auld guidwife's well-hoordit nuts
>   Are round and round divided,
> And mony lads' and lasses' fates
>   Are there that night decided;
> Some kindle, couthie, side by side,
>   And burn thegither trimly;
> Some start awa' wi' saucy pride,
>   And jump out-owre the chimly,
>   Fu' high that night.

> 'Jean slips in twa' wi' tentie e'e;
>   Wha' 'twas she wadna' tell;
> But this is Jock, and this is me,
>   She says in to hersel';
> He bleezed owre her, and she owre him,
>   As they wad never mair part;
> Till, fuff! he started up the lum,
>   And Jean had e'en a sair heart
>   To see't that night.'"

"What fun!" cried Lady Muriel. "Let us have some nuts, and try our fortune."

Well, we burnt my cousin Mary Grey and young Frank Henderson together, but they didn't like it all, and Frank bounced off the bar and into the grate; then we tried her sister Sophy and Paul Dedham, but it was no use—so we concluded that those two young people must pick up fresh admirers, or live and die old maids.

Then Muriel, who had been educated abroad and knew but little about old English customs, was initiated into the mysteries of ducking for apples, and eating one before the looking-glass, with a view to discover her future husband, who, it is believed, is seen peeping over her shoulder. Then we got talking about the other rites and ceremonies celebrated on Halloween; and I remembered that popular belief ascribed to children born on that night the possession of certain mysterious faculties, such as that of perceiving and holding converse with supernatural beings.

Sir Walter Scott, it will be recollected, makes use of this circumstance in his romance of *The Monastery*.

By-and-bye Mildred said, "How is it Mr. Montagu has not come? I thought you said, Fred, he would come to tea?"

"So I did. I met him on the Knightstone Road and gave him your invitation, and he said he certainly would come; but he's never to be depended upon. These business fellows never are."

"Is Mr. Montagu an old friend of yours?" Falconbridge asked; "I don't remember hearing you mention his name before?"

"No, I dare say not, yet he and I were at Ipswich Grammar School fifteen or twenty years ago, and I had quite lost sight of him till the other day, when he found us out. He's a Suffolk man, and one of those men who are making haste to be rich. He lives in the north of England, and is in the corn trade. I only hope he won't come to grief or ruin his health. He's safe to do one or the other, by over application to business," I added. "I remember him. It seems only yesterday, when we big fellows used to chaff little Gerard. He was a nice boy, though."

"Gerard Montagu—what a pretty, romantic name!" Muriel says, pensively.

"Yes, and his is a romantic history."

"Indeed, do tell us about it; I am quite curious."

"Well, Montagu is a good name, you know. There are the Montagus Dukes of Manchester and Earls of Sandwich, and Montagues Barons Rokeby, and there were, in the old days, Montagus Barons, Earls and Dukes of Montagu; the Montagues Earls of Halifax, besides the Montacutes (which is the original name) who were Earls of Salisbury in 1337. But I don't think Gerald lays claim to be descended from any of these, but only from an old knightly family in Suffolk, who once held large estates within eight or ten miles of Ipswich. I remember his showing me an old silver seal once, with some arms engraved thereon, which he took the trouble to tell me were, in the language of heraldry, *argent, three fusils in fesse gules*, and I afterwards found out (though he never told me) that they were the arms of the Montacutes, Earls of Salisbury, of Edward the First's reign. His father, on his deathbed, had given him this seal, which he said had been in the family over two hundred years, and that it was almost the only thing left that seemed to prove their descent. He told him, so Gerald said, that the lawyers had been to him more than once about some property, the heirs for which were wanted, but he had no proofs, and, being poor (he was chaplain to some hospital, I think), he had not the means to prosecute his claims; but he reminded Gerard that the day might come when he should be able to claim his own."

"Were the estates large?" Falconbridge asked.

"Worth four or five thousand a year, I should think."

"Hum, does Montagu pin much faith on the seal?"

"Why? How do you mean?" I enquired.

"Well, don't you know there are crowds of people who fancy that there are large estates somewhere to which they are the rightful heirs—if they could only prove it?"

"Ay, there's the rub."

"And then there's the statute of limitations, too; if any one has had undisputed possession for twenty or sixty years (which is it?) the estate is secured to the present possessor."

"How cruel of you, uncle, to talk so," Muriel puts in. "It's so romantic to fancy Mr. Montagu will recover the possessions his ancestors owned after a lapse, perhaps of centuries, and I like romance."

"I dare say you do, my dear; but facts are stubborn things, and I doubt if Mr. Montagu will have much chance of getting back the family estates, unless he has some better proof than an old seal to help him."

"Does he expect himself to be successful?" Falconbridge added, turning to me.

"Well, no; I don't fancy he thinks much about the matter. But what reminded me of it was an advertisement in the *Times* the other day, headed '*Heir-at-law wanted*;' and appended to the paragraph the significant phrase, '*If this should meet the eye of Geoffrey Montagu, or his next of kin, he is requested to apply at Mr. ——, solicitor,*' (I forget the name and address) '*where he may learn something to his advantage.*' I cut the paragraph out, and sent it to Montagu, at Darlington."

"But I thought Mr. Montagu's name was Gerard," Muriel suggests.

"Quite true; but his father's was Geoffrey."

"Well, did he go and see this lawyer?"

"Yes, he came south on purpose, so he told me yesterday

He's rather knocked up with over work, and anxiety, and, although he's been successful in one or two corn speculations, it's a queer time, he says, now. He's struggled hard for a long time, having been battling with the world ever since he left school, and his great idea is to buy back the family estates, if he cannot get them any other way."

"I am quite interested in your friend," Muriel says. "How stupid of him not to come to-night, and my birthday, too," she adds, with a pretty pout.

"Why, my dear child," Falconbridge answers, "Mr. Montagu must be over thirty, if he was at school with Beverley, and you are only sixteen."

"Over *thirty!* why he is quite *an old man*; no, I mean a middle-aged man," the little chatterbox cries, as she corrects herself, remembering that her dear uncle (as she fondly calls her guardian) is much older, and her reflections are scarcely complimentary to his age.

After a merry evening, thanks to my dear wife's good-natured efforts, we all separated; Mildred remarking, as she put a warm comforter round Lady Muriel's neck, and kissed her:—"Good night, dear, get home out of the snow as soon as you can (it was falling heavily at the time) and *don't dream of any future husbands to-night.*"

CHAPTER II.

LADY MURIEL'S DREAM, AND GERARD MONTAGU'S CONFESSION.

"MURIEL, Muriel, dear, get up!"

The speaker is Mrs. Vaux, who has gone into Lady Muriel's bed-room in her *sac de nuit*, looking more peculiar than picturesque.

No response.

"What can be the matter with the child, she will not wake? Margaret, do come and see if you can wake her: I never did see a girl in so sound a sleep in my life; and the house may be burned down over our heads," Mrs. Vaux continues.

"My lady, my lady!" the housemaid cries, and tries to rouse her without effect. "Law, ma'am, how she does sleep."

There had been an alarm of fire from some old maids over the way—fortunately, however, not founded on fact—at least it was only a chimney, and that was soon put out, but not before the neighbouring households were unnecessarily roused from their slumbers at five o'clock in the morning.

At length, peace being restored in the Crescent, and Mrs. Vaux's fears subsided in a measure, Muriel was left to her slumbers, which were so profound as to be almost death-like.

When they all came down to breakfast, Lady Muriel complained of headache.

"You slept well enough—or at all events sound enough," Mrs. Vaux said.

"Did I, dear aunt? I had *such* an odd dream. I dreamt I

was carried away against my will to a place very far away. It
was in England, though, because the people spoke English, and
looked like English. There was a broad, beautiful river, with
parks on either side of it, and trees right down to the water's
edge. But the land was covered with snow, and it all looked so
white, and glistening, and ghost-like, under the moon which was
shining overhead. I found myself suddenly close to a great
mansion. In the distance I could see quite clear in the moonlight
a large town with towers and spires. It seemed quite sheltered
by little hills, which rose at its back and sides, and appeared to
nestle at their base, and its streets to try and climb up their sides.
Once I was close to the town, and looking at it, and then I was
at the great house, and a young man came out and spoke to me.
He was so handsome; tall, and dark, with curly hair, and such
nice whiskers. I am sure I should know him again if I saw him,
and the town and the river. Well, then all was mist again, and
after a long time I came back. It was such an odd dream; quite
unlike other dreams."

"Well, my dear, I dare say, it was in consequence of all your
talk last night. John was telling me about your Halloween
doings."

"Perhaps it was Mr. Montagu I saw, aunt."

"Who is Mr. Montagu, Muriel?"

"Oh! don't you know?"

And then pretty fair-haired Lady Muriel told Mrs. Vaux all
about our hero.

Meanwhile that gentleman was taking a constitutional on the
new pier preparatory to breakfast. He had come down for a few
days to taste the briny odours at Weston-super-*Mud* (as some one
truly, though not very politely, named this now fashionable
watering place), not so much on account of the place itself, for
he was not a believer in the efficacy of iodine, said to be given

out of the oozy slime at low water, but principally on my account, as he found that I had taken a house there. I used to run up and down every day to Bristol, to my place of business. My wife told me when I got home that night that he was coming to take tea with us at seven o'clock (I always dined in Bristol), and mentioned incidentally that she had met him that morning when walking with Lady Muriel, and that he seemed much struck with her little ladyship. He was profuse in his apologies for not coming as he had promised the previous evening, but business had prevented him; "and your husband will tell you, Mrs. Beverley," he added, "that I make it a principle never to neglect business."

"Mr. Montagu," Margaret announces, as she ushers into the room a tall, dark, gentlemanly-looking man, about thirty years of age, perhaps a little more.

Little Ethel, our only child, aged two years, is sitting on the floor amusing us with her small gossip and pretty ways; but her mother, who is one of those matrons that does not care to bore her guests with her babies as some people do, signs to Margaret to take off the little imp, who at first looks defiant, but at length good-naturedly succumbs, and trots off laughingly after "Maddie," as she calls our housemaid. Gerard begs that the little one shall not be taken away on his account, as he is fond of children; but mamma is peremptory, and only after much entreaty promises that baby shall come back to say good night.

We were sitting silently round the fire after baby's departure.

"Well, Gerard, what are you dreaming about?" I said, observing that usually amusing bachelor gazing into vacancy, as sober as a judge, and quite as stupid looking.

"Well, I was thinking of your fair friend, Mrs. Beverley," he said, addressing my wife.

"Well, and what do you think of her, Mr. Montagu?"

"Me? Oh, I don't know; she has a very sweet face, I think. I like those oval faces, with large violet eyes, and hair that sometimes looks dark and sometimes fair. You don't often see that hair, I think; it looks as if it were intended to be black or brown, only some stray sunbeams have got caught in its silken meshes. Tell me about her, Fred, I admire the little Lady very much," he added.

"Well, first and foremost, she is only sixteen."

"Nonsense; she looks quite nineteen or twenty."

"Yes, I dare say she does to a stranger, for she has had a great deal of trouble."

"I think I understood you she was a lady of title?" Gerard said, turning to Mildred.

"Yes; her father was Lord Kilpatrick, but on his death the title went to a distant cousin, who lives in the north of England. The Earl died intestate, and his widow was left entirely unprovided for; but Lady Muriel has found a good friend in Capt. Falconbridge, who has adopted her, and no doubt on his death she will be very well off."

"Have her family taken no notice of her?"

"Not the slightest; indeed they scarcely know of her existence. I believe Lady Kilpatrick, considering herself neglected by them in her life, and being a proud woman, made Capt. Falconbridge (who was an old lover of hers, and was to have married her had she not been carried off suddenly) promise to have no communication with them if he could avoid it. Her name appears in *Burke*, and that is about all the connection her Ladyship has with the aristocracy; and, besides ourselves, they scarcely know a soul in Weston but the doctor and the clergyman of the parish," I added.

"Kilpatrick! I fancy I've heard that name before," Gerard remarks. "What is the second title?"

"Viscount Chelmondiston."

"Lord Chelmondiston! Of course I know the name. He was Captain in our Artillery Corps at Abbot Wrington."

"Indeed!"

"Yes, and a very nice fellow, though rather fast. I don't suppose he's more than twenty-three or so."

"What's he like?"

"Well, he's not at all like Lady Muriel."

"Don't suppose he is, for she takes after her mother, so I've heard Falconbridge say; and, besides, the relationship must be very remote. I've been told that the title went to a cousin about sixteen times removed."

"Nonsense, Fred," murmurs Mrs. Beverley, over her work.

"Well, my dear, I am sure the late Earl of Kilpatrick was a precious distant relative of the present one, who it is hoped is a better sort of fellow than he was."

Presently baby, who had been put to bed but resolutely refused to sleep, was brought down stairs in an unpleasant state of wakefulness, and not being one of the shy sort, immediately made overtures to Gerard, who seemed nothing loath to take her, much to her mother's delight, and he immediately rose a hundred per cent. in her estimation I could see. However, the young urchin persisted in flogging her doll to such an extent for some heinous offence against propriety (which it was thought dolls were not in the habit of committing), and otherwise became so obstreperous through Montagu's encouragement, that summary measures had to be resorted to, and the young tyrant removed from the scene of her labours in a state of howl.

"Baby's a great favourite with everybody," her mamma proudly says, "but Lady Muriel quite spoils her."

"Indeed," said Gerard. "Then who would not be spoiled? 'Tis a sweet face, the sweetest I have ever seen."

"Who's? Baby's?" Mildred asked.

"No. Your friend, Lady Muriel's."

"Oh! yes, she is pretty."

When we retired for the night Mildred said to me, "Fred, dear, I do believe it's a case of love at first sight."

"What between Gerard and the baby?"

"No, you great goose."

"Well, who then?"

"Why, Mr. Montagu, of course; can't you see he's fallen in love with Muriel?"

"Bosh! my dear; you women are all match-makers. It's all bosh."

"Well, he's a nice fellow; I like him; and how baby took to him!"

CHAPTER III.

CONFIDENCES. GERARD'S ADVENTURE.

A MARVELLOUS day for the 5th of November, a quiet, warm, lovely autumn day, and but for its shortness it might be mistaken for September.

Some one suggested that the weather was so fine we might all have a sail, and, as Montagu's stay would be short, and we ought to take advantage of every fine day, I gave myself a holiday, and we went with the party from the Crescent over to Brean Down, and roamed about the part where the new fortifications are being constructed. Gerard attached himself to Lady Muriel, who seemed pleased with his attentions.

"Do you despise trade?" he asked her.

"Despise *trade*! Oh, dear, no; why should I? Uncle's kindest friend, Mr. Beverley, is in trade. I think his firm are large brokers and exporters in Bristol."

"Well, you know that some people in your Ladyship's class do affect to despise it."

"I dare say they do. But I don't know anyone in my class, as you call it; and I'm sure I don't want to if they are all as cold and unkind as my father was to poor mamma;" and her little Ladyship dashed a tear away with a haughty effort at self-control and attempted concealment as painful recollections rose up in her mind.

"You do not despise business, Mr. Montagu, do you?" she presently inquired.

"No, I like it well enough when one has an object."

"And yours is a noble ambition, I think."

"Mine?"

"Yes, I think it is noble to strive to win back the old estates which have been in your family for centuries, and which have left you through no fault of your own."

"Do you?" Gerard said, and the colour mounted his cheek with mingled pride and pleasure as he looked at the sweet maiden walking by his side, and thought that for her sake it would be a worthy ambition to strive and to succeed.

"Mr. Beverley said you had had some communication with a London lawyer about those estates."

"Yes, I saw Mr. Grainger, and he seemed to think he could prove my claims; but of course I had to authorise him to proceed, and equally of course there were preliminary expenses. I don't know what to think about it. I ran down to Ipswich whilst in town, and took a cab over to the place, saw the church and the old hall, and took an impression of one or two of the brasses of my ancestors—one of Queen Elizabeth's and one of Charles the First's reign," he added.

"Is it a pretty place?"

"Very, for Suffolk, but, you know, nothing to compare with Somersetshire. The country about is undulating in some parts, but mostly very flat. The village of Montagu is much scattered, but the old church stands very well, near the high road,—the churchyard is bounded on two sides by the park, and the great avenue is close to the old grey tower, which looks very pretty seen through the vista of trees. The old hall was originally built by my family about the fourteenth century, though little remains of the original structure but the foundations, I suspect. The present edifice is decidedly Tudor in character, and was erected in the early part of Queen Elizabeth's reign."

"Well, I hope you will be successful," Muriel says warmly,

looking up in her frank, winning way into his face; "you have my best wishes, I'm sure."

"Thank you, Lady Muriel; there is nothing I should prize higher than your good wishes," Gerard replies earnestly.

"Indeed, you are too kind," Muriel says quickly; and with woman's instinct changes the subject, as if feeling she was getting on dangerous ground.

Gerard had seen a good deal of Lady Muriel the last few days.

We were so intimate with the Falconbridge household that scarcely a day passed but we were either at *theirs* or they at *ours*.

[That's pure Suffolk, the last phrase, I take it.]

When we got home they must needs make a day of it, and we all went in to tea at the Crescent; and Falconbridge, to please the young people (my cousins were there), let off a lot of fireworks; and Gerard must needs persuade Lady Muriel, who was fond of fun, and like all pretty maidens disposed to be a little flirt, to go outside and see them better. We left early, and I persuaded Falconbridge to walk down with us and have a smoke; and Mildred, having seen we were properly provided with the nicotian weed and the necessary pipes, left us to our fate.

"Well, Mr. Montagu," Falconbridge said, "Beverley here has been telling us about you being advertised for the other day in the papers. I hope something is likely to come of it."

"Thanks,—I don't know I'm sure; I'm beginning to disbelieve in old estates and old families."

"Indeed. Rather hard I think in the face of facts; but there's no doubt that the aristocracy of to-day were in too many cases the *parvenus* of yesterday; and the working man of the nineteenth century boasts in some instances the blood of the Plantagenets."

"Do you think so?"

"Sure of it. Why isn't it Burke, in his *Vicissitudes of Fami-*

lies, who tells us that there is living at this moment in Beaulieu, in Hants, a woodman who is the lineal descendant of one of the Plantagenet kings?

"Isn't the present representative of the great northern family, the Conyers, a postman at Hexham, or somewhere thereabouts? I knew an Irish baronet myself a pauper in a hospital in the north, and his next heir was one of the Irish constabulary.

"Then look back at the history of many of our aristocracy. One man's great grandfather was a grocer, became Lord Mayor of London, and got made a baronet. His son gets into Parliament, and is made a Peer when a new batch is wanted to swamp the Lords on some Liberal question. The present lord is twice as proud and haughty as a De Courcy, a Stanley, a Howard, or a Percy.

"Another noble lord's grandfather was a lawyer, and becomes Lord Chancellor; he marries his cook, and his grandson figures in the Divorce Court. Or perhaps the descendant of twenty earls, an *effete* gentleman who boasts of his blue blood obtained through marrying in and in for ten generations, until it has become, shall I say *ichor*, falls in love and marries a pretty actress, and the result is that the azure becomes more crimson, and the brains of the new generation are improved in quality, whilst the physical man is improved in tone. I've had some experience, and I say this, that in these days *money is everything*, blood and birth *nothing*.

"A man with money can aspire to any one!"

"By-the-bye, Gerard, I think you said you knew Lord Chelmondiston, Lady Muriel's relative," I put in.

"Well, I don't know much of him. The first time I met him, it was a queer business."

"You don't say so!"

"Yes, I do. I was then in business at South Wrington, and

was going home to Barton, where I lodged — about two miles off.

"Abbot Wrington is an old town in the north of England, standing on a peninsula, and jutting out into the sea. South Wrington, the new town, lies more back, and stretches away to the south, rather towards Barton, which is a little watering place, you know. There are large iron works at South Wrington, and at the time I speak of the men were out on strike. Some of them were desperate-looking fellows, and I often thought I would rather not meet any of them on a dark night. Well, I had been on drill (I was a full private in our Artillery Corps), and we strolled into the Royal Hotel afterwards, to have a smoke and a glass of grog before going home, for it was a cold night in December. Lord Chelmondiston had been on drill too; but, to tell the truth, he was rather a fast fellow at that time—it's now four years ago, he was only nineteen or twenty, and I dare say he's altered now. At any rate, he went off to the theatre with Menzies, one of our captains, and a great toady. Where they went afterwards I don't know, but I left the hotel a little before twelve, and was on my way home, when I heard the sound of some one riding furiously behind me. The tide was up, and I couldn't get by the sands, which were always covered at high water, and there was nothing for it but to go over the sand hills (or bents, as they call them in the north), which in the darkness was not pleasant; they are so full of pitfalls. I thought this fellow must either be mad or a fool, or he would not come pounding along at this pace such a night as this, and in such a place. However, he passed me at a gallop, yelling out as he went by a drunken 'Tally ho!'

"Fearing something would be sure to happen, I hurried after him as fast as I could, and I don't suppose I had gone another hundred yards before I heard a cry of 'Help!'

"Sure enough his Lordship is down, I thought. Lucky for him its soft sand and not hard boulder.

"I ran on as fast as I could, as I heard another cry; and, by Jove, there he was, pitched off the horse on to his head, and two fellows trying to rob him. I recognised one of them as a man I had seen at the Iron Works, and before he could say Jack Robinson I had given him a crack with the flat of my sword bayonet, which sent him down like a shot. The other fellow was off in quick sticks, and luckily we were not far from a lonely farm house, which stands midway between Barton and West Wrington, and I was able to get assistance and to take him in.

"His collar bone was out, but we got him removed in a few days to the Castle, and my dear old friend, Dr. Evans (a first-class fellow), attended him, and soon pulled him through. I think it did him good, you know; I don't believe he's been drunk since."

"Sharp lesson, certainly,—lucky that you were in the way, it strikes me," Falconbridge remarked.

"Was he going home?" I asked.

"Well, he *thought* he was, I suppose, but the fact is, if he had gone much farther he would have found himself in the German Ocean, I suspect."

"What became of the fellow you knocked down?" said Falconbridge.

"Oh, he? James Beard, I remember the fellow's name was. We picked him up; he was stunned, you know; and we took him in, and then sent off for a policeman.

"I had to appear against him at the assizes, and he got two years.

"He says '*he owes me one, and means to pay me some day,*'" he added.

"Did Lord Chelmondiston express himself as grateful to you?" Falconbridge asked.

"Oh, yes, he behaved like a brick, and has been very civil to me since then.

"Of course, the papers got hold of the story, but they told a lot of lies, praised me up no end, and said nothing about his Lordship's being drunk. They headed it 'Daring Highway Robbery'; and there was an illustration of course in the *Police News*, and didn't they make me handsome!"

As Gerard went back to his hotel that night he thought a great deal about what Falconbridge had said about birth, and blood, and money, and he resolved to himself this task: to win back the Montagu estates, and, if successful, to offer Lady Muriel his hand.

"She will not despise me because I'm a corn merchant," he said, "and Falconbridge is too much a man of the world to oppose it, if I can only make her love me. At any rate, if *I ever marry at all, Muriel shall be my wife.*"

CHAPTER IV.

AN INVITATION, AND WHAT CAME OF IT.

Six months have passed away, and the early summer days have come again.

Gerard soon returned to the North, after spending a very happy fortnight, so he said, at Weston-super-Mare: thanks to me, he observed, but my wife thought perhaps the thanks were more due to Lady Muriel.

I heard from him twice or thrice since, and he never failed to inquire particularly after her. He was getting on very well, I understood, but I could not help fancying he was overtasking his strength, and one day he would rue it.

He used to start from Darlington (where he had gone to reside, as being more central for his business) early in the morning, in time for Leeds corn market; and, after travelling almost all day and attending the sale, he would get home at six or seven o'clock quite done up, having probably tasted nothing since he left home in the morning. Three or four days in the week he was travelling, attending even the London market, and so, by his unremitting attention to business, was laying the seeds of disease in the race for wealth. He used to complain of his head a good deal, but he would say, when urged to take more rest, that a poor man must work—that bread was so hard to get now-a-days, and that he had an object in view, an ambition, which wealth alone would enable him to gratify.

Dr. Evans warned him that constant railway travelling had been proved to be most baneful—that it laid the train of brain diseases, besides affecting the health in other ways, and he would not answer for the results if Montagu persisted in sticking so close to business. Montagu only laughed at him, called him a jolly old humbug, and told him about Lady Muriel.

He was his dear friend, and so he confided in him, though perhaps he would not have told his secret to any one else in the world.

And Dr. Evans' face (which usually looked so grave and sad, as if he had troubles and trials which *he* could not confide to another) grew graver and sadder, and he went his way with a sigh on his lips and a pain at his heart.

Yes, it must be owned that our hero had fallen in love with charming Muriel Mandeville; and "absence only made his heart grow fonder," as Moore says.

Did Lady Muriel return his affection? Time alone will prove.

"Mother," Lord Chelmondiston said, strolling into her Ladyship's boudoir at Sneyd Park, Lord Kilpatrick's estate on the Orwell; "Mother, I met Montagu in town this morning; he's looking shockingly knocked up. It's such an age since I had seen him, that I was quite delighted. I met him in the Park, a most unlikely place to see him he told me, but he was so fagged with business that he had come out for an airing. I took him into the Junior Carlton, and gave him some lunch; he wouldn't come at first, but I may say I dragged him."

"My dear, I hope you did no such thing."

"Yes, I did, *figuratively*, of course."

"Well, dear," Lady Kilpatrick said, looking quite relieved to find that his lordship had not had recourse to physical force to induce his friend to accompany him to his club; "and what did Mr. Montagu say to you?"

"Oh, lots, mother. I believe he's knocking himself up with business. By the way, he said he had met a relation of ours at Weston last autumn."

"Impossible, Arthur."

"Quite true, mother, my cousin—Muriel Mandeville."

"Oh, the late Countess's daughter. What sort of a girl is she? Her mother was pretty, but she was a *governess*, I believe, designing I dare say, and no doubt *managed* to make your father's cousin marry her."

"That's a very unjust speech of yours, mother, and not like you," her son replied indignantly.

"Well, dear," Lady Kilpatrick said pleasantly, "perhaps you are right, but you have not answered my question."

"Oh, Montagu says 'she's lovely, she's divine,' and all that sort of thing;—fact is, I believe he's in love with her."

"Nonsense, Arthur."

"Well, mother, and why shouldn't he? If her own relations take no notice of her, I don't see why other people shouldn't.

"I declare," the young Lord went on, "I was quite ashamed of myself when I thought I did not know my own cousin—who was living amongst strangers, because her own kith and kin forget the ties of relationship.

"Besides, if it comes to that, we ought to be very thankful to her for being a girl."

Her Ladyship burst out laughing.

"Well, you may laugh, mother,—but if Lady Kilpatrick had had a son instead of a daughter—father would have been plain Mr. Mandeville, and you would *not* have been Countess of Kilpatrick."

Her Ladyship was silent; the shaft had gone home.

Lord Chelmondiston saw his advantage, and pressed it.

"Mother, don't you think it would be kind to ask Muriel to come and see us?"

"Well, Arthur, I really don't know, I will think about it.

"And now, dear boy, you must leave me, for it is half-past seven, and I must dress for dinner."

"I say, mother, Montagu says Captain Falconbridge, with whom Muriel lives, is fifty if a day, and looks ever so much older," the young fellow returned to remark, and then he left his mother to her own reflections.

Her Ladyship did think about it, and the more she thought about it the more it seemed to her that they had acted unkindly to Lady Muriel.

It is true that they had written once to her since her mother's death—but her letter, she admitted, was not calculated to make a very good impression. They had somehow looked down upon Muriel's mother because she was not born in the purple—but what did they know about her? Nothing! She was a perfect lady, every one said that, and her only crime was her poverty, which, coupled with the fact that she had won Lord Kilpatrick's heart, who every one knew was a scamp—was sufficient for what —to make the relatives of her child neglect her as if she were basely born.

Then, too, there was this attachment of Mr. Montagu's—there might be no truth in it—but if there were, what then, who was to blame? If Lady Muriel married out of her circle it would certainly be the fault of the family. Mr. Montagu was a very worthy young man,—very worthy indeed;—they owed him a debt of gratitude for saving Arthur's life;—but still Lady Muriel must not be suffered to marry a corn merchant. She would invite Muriel to come and see them at Sneyd Park,—and she should accompany them to their place in Ireland, Castle Court, where she was born,—she should be introduced to people in her own sphere of life,—and this dream (if there were any dreaming on her part) should pass away as all dreams do.

Having satisfied herself as to her goodness of heart in thinking of the poor orphan—(she would have been the last to admit that family pride and *noblesse oblige* had anything to do with it)—her

Ladyship resolved to invite Muriel to Sneyd Park—and Lord Kilpatrick offering no objection (he never did) a missive was sent to Weston-super-Mare accordingly.

It came a day or two after the conversation between mother and son related above, and it found John Falconbridge sitting on the sands, and Lady Muriel near him, reading *Lothair*.

"Uncle, are all the great people beautiful and talented, as Mr. Disraeli describes them?"

"Oh, Disraeli sees the aristocracy and their surroundings through rose coloured spectacles. The book is clever—but if we had had a few ugly peers, plain and stupid peeresses, and less about Ayranism, Semitic races, and Theodoras—the book would have been more realistic, certainly more readable."

"I should like to know more about the people he describes, uncle—to judge for myself."

"Would you," he said, and looked at her curiously.

"I've had a letter, would you like to see it?"

"Yes, dear, if you like."

"It's from Lady Kilpatrick!"

John Falconbridge started and turned pale, but collecting himself, said sadly,

"I suppose it's to ask you to go there?"

"Why, how did you guess that?"

"I've long had a presentiment that they would."

"They ask me to go and make a long visit; isn't it kind of Lady Kilpatrick? I am so happy."

Then suddenly she looked up and saw the big tears in his eyes, and she stole her pretty little hand into his big broad palm, and was silent.

"Well, dear, and you will go of course?"

"No, not for worlds, uncle, if you do not wish it. You have been a father to me. I owe everything to you, and no one shall take me from you."

"Ah, my dear, I am afraid they will; and if they should, I think it would break my heart to lose you."

John Falconbridge was, however, too unselfish to stand in the way of Muriel's happiness. A week afterwards Muriel was at Sneyd Park.

She had never been in this part of the country before, though when she returned from school in Germany it was intended she should come by one of the Great Eastern boats to Harwich, but her illness prevented, and she afterwards came the Calais and Dover route. Yet somehow the scene was strangely familiar. The beautiful river, the view of its great curves from the Hall, the distant town of Ipswich, all seemed like some picture she had seen, some vision of the place she had seen long ago.

Lady Kilpatrick came out and greeted her warmly. Lord Chelmondiston, who had intended meeting her at the station, came in soon after, and she could not help remarking to Lady Kilpatrick when they were introduced,

"It all seems very odd, but if I did not know to the contrary, I should be quite positive that I had seen Lord Chelmondiston before."

"Say Arthur, please," that young aristocrat put in with his most fascinating smile; "you know we are cousins, but it is strange, I seem to feel that I have seen *your* face before."

Muriel laughed a merry laugh, and remarked that "her face was by no means an uncommon one."

Her dark handsome cousin was about to make a very complimentary answer, for the lady was pretty, and he was an intense admirer of pretty women, but Lady Kilpatrick carried away her young relative to take off her things.

She enjoyed her visit very much. Lady Kilpatrick was not a bad sort of woman, and she soon got to be fond of the sweet, even-tempered, clever girl who had come amongst them. There were lots of people there, and Muriel saw plenty of company. After staying a month or two the Countess's quick eye discerned something which made her think that her son had certainly fallen in love with his pretty cousin, and she was by no means sure that the feeling was not reciprocal. She certainly had not bargained for this, but Lord Chelmondiston had been rather fast, and it would be as well, now that he was twenty-four, that he should think of settling down.

Lady Muriel was only seventeen, and perhaps, after all, there might be nothing in it. Besides, how about Mr. Montagu? She never had been able to make anything out about that. Muriel had once or twice mentioned him, but it was in such a way that one would not have thought there was any feeling in that quarter. At any rate matters must take their course; it would be time enough to interfere when interference became necessary. Perhaps if she were to speak now, she might only put ideas into their heads which were not there before.

So her Ladyship said nothing.

One day they took Lord Kilpatrick's yacht and sailed down the Orwell and up the Stour. There was a party of five or six, but somehow or other Lord Chelmondiston and Lady Muriel seemed to have so much to say to each other as to have little time to devote to their guests. Somebody said something about old customs, and Halloween came up in the course of conversation, which reminded Muriel that her birthday was on that day. Lord Chelmondiston bent over her and said,

"Muriel, shall I tell you a secret?"

"What is it?"

"Well, of course you won't believe it?"

"How do you know?"

"Well, last October we had some Irish people, the Bourchiers, at the Hall, and they taught me a Halloween spell. I tried it, and sat up all night to watch the result.

"I declare to you most solemnly that you *walked into the Hall, and I saw you the same as I saw you when first you came to us.*

"You stayed a minute or two and then you vanished as you came. I was sorry I had attempted to tamper with the powers of the unseen world, but if I were on my oath before a court of justice, I should swear it."

Muriel blushed, and then seemed a little frightened.

"Do you not believe me?"

"I don't know," she said.

"Do you know what it meant?"

"No!"

"It meant you were to marry me."

"How silly you are, Arthur," Muriel said, and then she went to the other end of the yacht and joined the others.

CHAPTER V.

DE MORTUIS.

THE end of last July Gerard came in upon us at Weston quite unexpectedly. Mildred was shocked at his appearance, for he looked haggard to a degree, and almost wild at times.

He had lost a great deal of money lately through some unfortunate ventures, and he had been to his lawyer in London about the estates, and evidently had not received good news, though for some days he was taciturn, almost morose, when we approached the subject. He had heard that Lady Muriel was at Sneyd Park, but seemed to expect that she would have been home again ere this.

My wife was distressed about him. He didn't seem to know what to do with himself—he was always going in and out, but he seemed restless and not himself at all. He was very anxious to hear everything about Muriel, how her relatives treated her, how she liked her cousin, and above all when she was coming back!

My wife had her suspicions, from certain letters she had received from the little lady, that all was not as it should be, and Gerard's chance was small; but she had no opportunity of saying anything, because he neither made her nor me his confidante in the matter.

The last night he was with us (I had gone down to Falconbridge's for a quiet smoke, as he was rather lonely in Muriel's absence) he seemed more hopeful, Mildred thought, but he was bewailing his poverty, and wondering how it was poor men ever got married.

"Well," Mildred said, "I suppose it all depends upon whether people love each other very much, but if people marry when they are poor the love must not be all on one side."

"Well, I've nothing to marry on now," he said.

Then Mildred answered quietly, whilst she took little Ethel on her knee, and was apparently busying herself in fastening baby's shoe —

"It would not be honourable, would it, for any one to propose if they had not enough to live on?

"Now, baby dear, I will sing you one of your own little nursery rhymes, and Mr. Montagu shall listen to us, shan't he, dear?" and she warbled to baby, much to that little innocent's delight, who tried to join :—

> "There was a little man, and he wooed a little maid,
> And he said, 'Little maid, will you wed, wed, wed?
> I have little more to say. Then will you? yea or nay;
> For least said is soonest mended —ded, ded, ded.'
>
> "The little maid replied, some say a little sigh'd,
> 'But what shall we have for to eat, eat, eat?
> Will the love that you're so rich in, make a fire in the kitchen?
> Or the little God of Love turn the spit, spit, spit?'"

When Montagu rose to go he said —

"Good bye, Mrs. Beverley. Baby has taught me a lesson to-night. I shall not forget it."

A month afterwards I received a letter from his great friend, Dr. Evans, which shocked us all very much.

It ran as follows :—

"Darlington, 31st August, 1870.

"My Dear Mr. Beverley,—

"I am sure you will be very grieved to hear that our mutual friend, Montagu, is no more.

"He died on the 28th of this month, in the Lunatic Asylum at York. I had long feared that his brain was becoming affected, and warned him not to overtask his strength, but it was unavailing. Almost immediately after his return from the South a marked change was observed in him. It began by his fancying that he was always followed about by a man whom he was instrumental in bringing to justice some years ago in a highway robbery case. Then he got a scheme into his head, and went about for signatures to get an Act of Parliament passed about some estates near Ipswich, which he said were his.

"The poor fellow had been prosecuting his claims for some time, and it was thought he was approaching a successful issue, when his lawyer discovered that although he was the undoubted heir, the last purchaser had, about a hundred years ago, suspecting some flaw in the title, protected himself by a special Act of Parliament. Montagu had paid something like £1,000 to this man, and all to no purpose.

"Then, poor fellow, it appears he had formed an attachment to a young lady in the South, living somewhere near you, as I understood, and from what transpired during his stay at Weston he gathered that his hopes were at an end in that quarter. This, together with the losses in business he had recently sustained, preyed upon his mind to that extent that, fearing he would do violence to himself, we took him to York.

"Strange to say, when we got to the Asylum he was to all appearances as sane as you and I; so much so indeed that the doctor, turning to us, said pleasantly, after a pause, 'And which, gentlemen, is the patient?' Then he laughed in our faces, accused us of conspiring to shut him up; and we were obliged to take him home again. Soon, however, he had a recurrence of the attack, he was removed to the Asylum, grew rapidly worse, and succumbed at last. I have lost a good friend in poor Gerard

Montagu, who was universally liked and respected here, and as you may suppose his death has made a painful impression in this neighbourhood. I should add that I found amongst his papers a little packet, which I enclose, addressed to Lady Muriel Mandeville. As I do not know her ladyship's address, may I beg you to give it her?—Yours truly,

"GEORGE MOORE EVANS."

Mildred could not help weeping when she heard the distressing news, and I was also very much cut up.

Ethel (who was her mother's almost constant companion), seeing the tears in her eyes, cried too, out of sympathy, as children do; but, poor thing, she cannot understand why her kind friend never comes now; and she often asks her mother when "good Midder Montadu," as she called him, is coming again. It is a trite saying, but a true one, that misfortunes never come singly. My dear friend Falconbridge never seemed himself after Muriel left, and I was alarmed to find him in a fit one night when I strolled in to have my accustomed cigar with him.

We telegraphed immediately for Lady Muriel, who came late the next evening, too late, however, to see him alive.

Poor little dear, she was dreadfully distressed when she found her dear guardian was no more. My wife thought she would be really ill; it seemed to have such an effect upon her.

It was not for some days that we dared to break to her the news of Gerard's sat fate. She had a kind, warm heart, and wept tears of sympathy when Mildred read Dr. Evan's letter to her.

I don't think she had any idea of the depth of Gerard's affection for her. He had been too honourable to say one word, until he felt he should be in a position to offer her marriage. But she took the little packet, opened it, and found therein a beautiful emerald ring.

"Will you not wear it for his sake?" Mildred said, "it can do you no harm."

"Oh, yes,—if I may;—if *he* will let me."

Mildred looked up askance, and saw pretty Muriel's face suffused with blushes.

Mildred went up to her and whispered something.

Muriel blushed and smiled.

"I am so glad, dear."

"What does it all mean?" I asked.

"Nothing, dear."

I afterwards learnt that there was a sort of tacit understanding between Muriel and somebody else; and about a month after the *Morning Post* announced that—

"An alliance was contemplated between Lord Chelmondiston, only son of the Earl and Countess of Kilpatrick, and his cousin, Lady Muriel Mandeville."

THE END.

AUTUMN.

The autumn waxeth old,
    The sun sets o'er the sea;
His golden rays so cold,
    So cold they shine on me.

The warmth of the summer sun
    Has gone with the summer leaves;
And the glory of the year went by
    When the reapers bound their sheaves.

Then the bearded grain was full,
    As the sickle cut it down;
Whilst the flowers of earth had faded,
    That on mossy banks had grown.

The autumn winds blow cold;
    And grey clouds dim the sky;
The wild blasts tell the dreary tale,
    That winter draweth nigh.

The giant lords of the forest,—
    The grand, the olden trees,—
Lowly they bend their heads to hear
    The whispering of the breeze.

The swallow southward flies,
    And dead leaves flutter and fall;
Golden and crimson they cover the ground,
    Like a splendid funeral pall.

The ocean is cover'd with foam,
    For the storm-king reigns around;

And the dreary roar of the soughing waves,
   Disturbs the peace profound.

And the glittering dew-drops lie
   Unquench'd in the morning light;
And all Nature seems to die,
   With its myriad forms so bright.

But the spring-tide comes again,
   With its verdure and its flowers;
And Nature shall again rejoice,
   Through the live-long summer hours.

A THOUGHT ON A SUMMER SEA.

When the golden sun is sinking
   Down beneath the western sea,
Oft there comes a solemn, silent,
   Brooding calm of mystery.

And the night shades, slowly creeping
   Up and over all the main,
Cover up the old world softly,
   So she goes to sleep again.

Then the stars shine out so sweetly,
   Sadly o'er the quiet scene,
Till the glimmering, gleaming twilight,
   Comes and drowns them in its sheen.

So they shut their bright eyes slowly
   Very slowly, one by one;
And the earth awaits the coming
   Of her sovereign lord the sun.

ERNEST BLAKE:

A CHRISTMAS STORY.

My father was a poor surgeon in the city of Gloucester, where he was both liked and respected, and his loss was much lamented. I was left an orphan very young, when I was scarce twelve years old. Our large and hitherto happy family party was broken up, and my brothers and myself sent out to make our fortunes in the world, friendless and alone. Not altogether friendless, though; for my uncle Joseph, who was a banker in Edinburgh, got both my brothers into the navy (they were just thirteen and fourteen when they entered), and, when I left school, some two years after, took me into the bank in Edinburgh, where I have since remained. My three sisters were taken charge of by another uncle, a lawyer in Gloucester, possessed of some means: the husband of a beautiful wife, very much younger than himself, but not the father of a family. I had been some three years in the bank, had many friends in the north, and, what was equally pleasant to a prudent man, had saved a little money, and was now in the receipt of (for a young man) a tolerable income. Perhaps I am a little romantic and superstitious—I rather think I must be; for, when Christmas came round this year—it was 1856—I felt that I must go down to Gloucester, to see my sisters, and that something of great consequence to myself would happen there. Uncle Joseph gave me a week's holiday, a large hamper of Scotch cakes and other sweetmeats, and a box containing some pretty Christ-

mas presents for my sisters and the family at Coatham House—
that was the name of our adopted home—and sent me off on my
journey.

I always like to go by the night mail, and so started by the
5.55 train, which would carry me through to London by half-
past ten on the following morning. I had some business in
town: I could finish it during the day, and, as time more than
money was the object, I could soon dash down to Gloucester by
the Great Western, and be with my sisters by ten or eleven that
night. I marked out my time in this way; and the evening of
Tuesday, the 22nd of December, saw me comfortably ensconced
in a first-class carriage prepared for my night journey to the
south. Our compartment was full all the way to Newcastle,
where the other passengers got out, leaving me alone; and I
hoped to remain undisturbed for the rest of my journey—as it
was now eleven o'clock, and I wanted to get a quiet sleep—till I
got to London. However, I was doomed to disappointment;
for, scarcely had the door closed after the retreating passengers,
and I had comfortably settled myself back for a nap, than a
gentleman and lady entered the carriage, and as the guard came
round to examine the tickets I saw "London" on theirs. The
gentleman—whom I at first mistook for a clergyman, but who
turned out to be a barrister, on the northern circuit—looked at
me earnestly as he entered: and I at him, for there was some-
thing about the man that took my fancy; and he also appeared
to be satisfied after his scrutiny. Tall and commanding in figure,
with hair and beard like Hamlet's father, "a sable silvered,"
and with a *tout ensemble* that bespoke high breeding, Mr. Vernon
was just such a man as I could like; and, as for his daughter (he
called her Annie, and I soon found out the relationship) she was
one of those beings who seem like angels in disguise sent to earth
on missions of love and mercy. It must be owned that I am an

ardent admirer of the sex, and certainly here admiration was not misplaced. I cannot describe now how she was habited, but it was in a dark dress, with a white burnous cloak on, that I first saw Annie Vernon, with such sunny ringlets half escaping from the charming little bonnet, which shielded her fair face, and with such sweet blue eyes and lovely Grecian features, dainty hands, and charming figure, as I shall never forget. There was a certain pallor on her cheeks that made me sigh for her, and at times a haggard expression about the face, which spoke of frequent pain and sometimes agony. I noticed all this in a glance, and it was quite sufficient to interest me in the young lady and her father, and I think we all improved upon acquaintance.

We had travelled as far as York, and had all of us taken a little refreshment there. Miss Vernon took a cup of hot coffee, and presently complained that it and the cold night wind had brought on an attack of neuralgia, a complaint from which it appeared she had long suffered. Again the haggard, weary look came o'er that fair face, and I longed to relieve her from her suffering. Have you ever read, gentle reader, Dr. Gregory's *Letters to a Candid Enquirer?* because, if you have not, read them at once. I had read the work, and had been introduced to Dr. Gregory himself, who was, at the time I speak of, Professor of Chemistry at the University of Edinburgh, and had imbibed the doctrines and philosophy of Mesmer when very young. Of late, too, I had experimented a good deal in animal magnetism, and to a certain extent studied the science ever since I left school, with what success the reader has yet to learn. I had frequently thrown "subjects" into the magnetic sleep, and had cured such slight maladies as trouble the teeth and head upon more than one occasion. So I thought that mesmerism might relieve his daughter, and accordingly asked Mr. Vernon if there were any objections to my throwing the young lady into the magnetic sleep in order to take away the pain which seemed, at times, as if it would overcome her.

"Oh no," said he, "I have seen enough of mesmerism to believe in it, and shall be glad, indeed, if you can be of any service to Annie."

"Trust me, I will do my best, if only the young lady will submit?" was my reply; and, Miss Vernon having no objection, I at once commenced operations. I had learnt their names from the label on their luggage, and their relationship from Mr. Vernon's observations.

"And now, if you please, Miss Vernon," I began, "you must be content for the next half hour or so to submit to my will; have no fears for yourself; I will not harm you; your father can interfere if he thinks proper. Look in my eyes steadily—so: do not blink or shut your eyes at all till you are forced to do so, and, once closed, do not attempt to open them again till I tell you."

"Very well, I will do as you bid," replied she; "only take away this dreadful pain."

It was wonderful how friendly we had become within the last hour or two; but then you see we had been talking all the way down from Newcastle, and had become quite intimate already. Whirling along at thirty miles an hour in the dead of night, with no sound save the thud-thud of the carriage wheels rattling over the metal rails at terrific speed, puffing and snorting, the iron horse prances onwards through the night air, drawing at his back, besides his living freight, ten thousand written thoughts addressed to friends and kinsmen hundreds of miles away. Meanwhile, I am sitting gazing earnestly and fixedly into Annie's sweet blue eyes, and waving my hands before her steadily and slowly. In measured time I beat the air, whilst pouring as it were the magic anodyne down over her yielding form. At length the eyelids droop, the hand relaxes its grasp, the whole form seems to lose its active power, the head falls against the cushioned back of the carriage, the eyes close, and she is asleep. I still continue for a minute or two to make the passes, for though all pain has gone, I want "to make assurance doubly sure," by deepening the sleep. At length I pause.

Mr. Vernon remarks: "How very extraordinary!"

I smile in triumph at having so soon accomplished my object.

"Have you ever seen anything of clairvoyance, Mr. Vernon?" say I—"and may I ask you, has Miss Vernon ever been mesmerised before?"

"To your first query, no. I have seen little of mesmerism except in the mere ordinary phenomena, and to the other, not to my knowledge. Indeed, I don't think my daughter has ever heard much about the science."

"Well then, sir, I shall, with your permission, endeavour to call out the clairvoyant faculty, which I think your daughter, Miss Vernon, possesses: perhaps you may see what is extraordinary indeed."

"Miss Vernon, are you asleep?" I ask.

There is no response.

"Answer me," I say authoritatively, at the same time slighty touching the organs of individuality and firmness, and pointing at the eyes (this commands obedience).

"Ye-es," at length gasps out the lady, in a manner and tone exactly opposite to her usual way of speaking.

"Do you see?" I ask.

Again the pause, and again the same hesitation of speech, as if she were tongue-tied.

I make a few rapid upward passes over the mouth, and she answers readily, "No."

"Then I command you to see," and with that I draw from my coat a steel rod, and point it first to her eyes, then to her lips, and then to her heaving bosom; she bounds as if a dart of flame had pierced her heart, and then falls back, in a trance-like state, and remains still and motionless.

How lovely and yet how weird-like she looked just then, as she lay back against the rich dark cushions of the carriage, with her fair golden curls in wild confusion falling down over her neck and shoulders, and contrasting strangely with the sombre hue of her dress, and the darkened half-hid shapes round her, just visible through the obscurity. The lamp was burning low, and gleamed fitfully and luridly down upon us all, sometimes leaving us in almost total darkness, and then throwing out one sickly yellow ray, which caused fantastic shapes to dance before our eyes, and brought out the shadowed outline and pale face of the sleeping beauty like some ghostly visitant doomed thus to appear. All was still and silent as the grave within, and an expression of unearthly beauty and spiritual intelligence had settled on her countenance; the roses stole back for an instant to her cheeks, and then disappeared, and she seemed listening and looking at sights and sounds perchance thousands of miles away. So, then, I touched her eyes, and bade her speak.

"Can you now see?" I repeat.

"Yes!" is the reply, and then I pause to ponder for a little time to collect my scattered thoughts.

Mr. Vernon cries, "Annie, do you see me?"

No answer.

"*Can* she not see?" he asks of me.

"No, indeed, nor hear either, unless placed *en rapport* with you. At this moment the lady can neither see nor hear, except I will it, and by my transferring, as it were, a portion of my power to another," I reply.

"Impossible!"

"It is even as I say, and I give you free leave to shout as lustily as you can. Miss Vernon will be quite unconscious of what you are doing."

Just at this moment we were entering a tunnel, and the engine gave a loud shrill whistle of warning as we dashed through; but Miss Vernon remained with as placid and unruffled a countenance as if the stillness of night reigned profound—not a muscle moved, and there was not the slightest indication of consciousness.

"Are you satisfied now, Mr. Vernon?" I ask.

He bows acquiescence, and I proceed with my manipulations.

Having placed them *en rapport*, as it is called: "Miss Vernon, who is this?" I ask.

"My papa."

"What is his name?"

"LORD Vernon!"

I look round to Mr. Vernon, enquiringly. He starts, turns slightly pale, and says,

"My daughter is certainly giving me a title to which I cannot say I have no right, but which I certainly do not bear at present; but I will tell you, if you care to hear, all about it some day."

"Perhaps it may be that Miss Vernon sees what you will become," I suggest, "and so addresses you by a title you may some day bear."

"Heaven knows; I have had a great deal of trouble about it; but ask her if she knows anything?"

"Miss Vernon, why do you call your father *Lord* Vernon?"

"Because he *is* Lord Vernon, or at least, can establish his claim to that title."

"How so?" Mr. Vernon asks.

"Why, my lord" (he looks pleased and smiles at this style of address), "I see some papers."

"Where?"

"At Mr. Soanes'."

"The family solicitor," he explains to me.

"What are they?"

"One, a very old parchment, written over in curious characters, and one in some foreign language—Latin, I think."

"Is it signed?"

"Yes."

"By whom?"

"Shall I spell it?"

"Yes."

"E-d-v-a-r-d-u-s IV., Edward the Fourth."

"It is," explains Mr. Vernon, "the patent conferring the title of Baron upon my ancestor, or, what is more probable, a copy of it, and a document I have long been searching for, but hitherto without avail."

"What other papers do you see?"

"One which looks like a certificate of some kind, and two or three folded up together."

"Can you see the names, if there are any, in the certificate?"

"Yes; John and Margaret Vernon."

"How very extraordinary," says Mr. Vernon to me; "I do believe, Sir, that this is the very certificate of marriage between an ancestor of mine and a certain fair lady about whose origin or antecedents I have been hitherto unable to gather anything. I verily believe that this will make my evidence complete before the Committee of Privileges of the House of Lords."

The fact was, as I afterwards learned, that Mr. Vernon was a claimant for an old baronage created in 1470, and which had been in abeyance since 1760, when the 13th Lord had died, leaving five daughters, who were, of course, equal claimants for the title and estates. The patent was made out, as almost all the old titles were, for the heirs-general, instead of being limited to the "heirs male of his body lawfully begotten," as they have it now-a-days; and, in consequence, the law was that the title should remain in abeyance till the descendants of four of the sisters had all died off, when the family which remained, if they could make good their claim, would become the possessors of both title and estates. Diligent enquiry had been made for many years, and it had been proved that the families of three of the sisters had become extinct. About the fourth there was no certainty; but more of that anon. Mr. Vernon's telling me this reminded me that my mother's name was Vernon; and I should remark here, by the way, with reference to the *name* being retained through female descendants, that Mr. Vernon told me it was ordered in the old Lord's will that, if either of his daughters married, their husbands should take the name of Vernon; and a certain sum was left to pay the necessary fees required on obtaining a "sign manual" for that purpose.

Mr. Vernon was overjoyed upon hearing that the missing documents which were so essential to prove his claim were safe, feeling sure they would be found. Nor was he disappointed, for, sure enough, there they were, in an old oak chest in the lawyer's office, hid away snug from the light for this many a day, and now only discovered through the wonderful faculty of clairvoyance.

I had often seen clairvoyance before, and had once or twice succeeded in eliciting it myself, but never with so complete success as upon this occasion; and I was so delighted with what I had witnessed, that I determined to put to the test these inborn powers of Miss Vernon, and endeavour to produce some of those phenomena which mesmerists classify under the names of "introvision" and "prevision," or prophecy.

And here, gentle reader, I must tell you a secret. Long years ago, when I was quite a boy, I had fallen in love with a young lady who lived near Gloucester, and whose father was a retired officer in the army, living on his half pay and some little private property which had been left to him. Major de Courcy was a proud man—proud of his birth, for he represented a cadet branch of one of the oldest families in the realm, and proud of his position. He was looked up to in Gloucester as one of its chief citizens, and might have been elected any time these ten years mayor of that ancient city. Mrs. de Courcy was one of the most fascinating women I ever beheld, and one of the best, too; and, as for the daughter—oh! how I loved her. Amy de Courcy was an only daughter, possibly a little spoilt, but she was such a graceful creature, with hair of light brown, and beautiful grey eyes (Sir Joshua Reynolds says grey eyes are the most expressive), a swan neck, and sylph-like figure, that would have rivetted the gaze and commanded the admiration of the most confirmed misogynist. I had been almost always away at school, so seldom saw her, and for many a year was in love with Amy simply because she was my ideal of perfection. My boyish affection had almost died away—at least I thought so; and yet I still wore round my neck a little locket, with one tiny ringlet of her beautiful hair enshrined therein. I had seldom seen her of late years, and knew that she did not care for me as much even as for her pet Persian cat; and, indeed, for that matter, it would have been strange indeed if my affection had been reciprocated, we were so nearly strangers to each other.

But to return. I said I wanted to put to proof those wonderful tales about clairvoyant's gifts of foresight, and telling by certain media what was happening to certain persons. So, whilst Mr. Vernon was taking down his notes, I took out my little locket, placed it in Miss Vernon's hand, and bade her tell me what it was.

"It is a locket," she replied, wearily, after pressing it to her forehead, to which it appeared the organ of sight had fled. I made some energetic passes over her, and she seemed to imbibe fresh vigour with each wave of the hands, and to increase in intelligence with each downward sweep, as I poured the magnetic fluid upon her.

"Whose hair is this?" I asked, "tell me what you see?"

Presently, after holding the locket, as before, to her forehead, and with a great effort, as if straining after something, she replied,

"I see an old mansion, with a large and ancient gateway, a church at one side, and a great avenue of trees up to the house."

"Well, and what else? Who is there?"

"Some ladies and an old gentleman."

"Do you see a young lady there?"

"Yes."

"Who is she?"

"It is the young lady to whom this hair belongs."

"Good."

I paused for a moment, and then said, hurriedly and low,

"Can you look into her heart, and tell me if she loves any than herself?"

Do not sneer, gentle reader, clairvoyance is sometimes all but omniscient!

"She is very fond of her mother."

"How can you tell?"

"I see her constantly looking at her, and, sometimes, when no one is near, she goes up and kisses her."

"Well, but does she love any one else? Has she any lover?" I ask excitedly.

"I cannot tell," she murmurs in reply, wearily.

"But you must, I command you," and with that I again drew out my steel wand and touched her.

Instantly she darted forward, and then fell back for a moment, as if electrified, recovered herself and murmured "No."

Inexpressibly relieved at what I have heard, I proceed with my questions.

"What are they talking about?" I ask.

"An elder lady, her mother, is speaking to her."

"Well, listen to what they say."

"She says that she has received a letter from Miss Blake, saying that her brother Ernest"——

"Yes, I am Ernest Blake; well, go on."

"That Ernest comes home for a few days at Christmas, and they would like to bring him over to see them."

"Well, what does Amy say?" I am sure it is Amy.

"She says, 'Let them come here.'"

"Well, and shall I go?"

"Yes."

It is enough, I am more than satisfied.

"Now, Miss Vernon, I have fatigued you much, and you shall sleep—sleep soundly for a few hours, until we get to town."

With that I motioned Mr. Vernon what I was going to do, and with a few rapid passes threw my patient into a deep sleep, from which I knew she would awake refreshed and well.

So then she slept. Five hours afterwards she awoke refreshed, and quite recovered: quite oblivious of all that had passed since I had put forth the charm of "woven paces and of waving arms," and robbed her of all consciousness. Mr. Vernon briefly thanked me for the marvels I had disclosed to him, and for curing his daughter, for the time being, at least, of that most painful nervous disease, tic doloreux; whilst I had to thank him for his kindness in allowing me to experiment upon so fair a subject as his daughter. We then dozed away till we got near London, and chatted to each other during the rest of the journey, I promising to visit them when next in Newcastle. And when I left my two companions, after awakening Miss Vernon, it was with feelings of something like pain. I had only known them twelve hours, but then twelve hours in a carriage all to yourselves, and with young people especially, is quite sufficient to make an agreeable acquaintance, that may afterwards ripen into a lasting friendship. I may here add that Miss Vernon's affliction never returned again. I soon finished my business in London, and was in Gloucester within a few hours, received with such generous hospitality by my jolly good-natured uncle and his charming wife —not to mention my sisters—as quite satisfied me of their tender regard for my welfare and continued interest in their nephew.

"And now, if you please, Mr. Ernest," says my eldest sister, in her capitally assumed prim way, "you are to go with me (or with us rather, for we have since determined all to go) to Anham Court to see the de Courcy's; they have kindly invited us to go up there where they are staying for a short time, to-morrow."

"Of course you will go, dear," Ethel says.

Ethel is my youngest sister, and I think I am fondest of her— at least I make her my confidante, and tell her all the state secrets, of which everybody else is supposed to be ignorant; but somehow or other I think they all know.

"Of course, Ethel," I say gallantly, "if *you* say so I go."

"But *Ethel* is not the attraction, Ernest, is she?" Bella puts in, giving a glance at me at the same time, intended to convey that she knows all about it.

"My sister's company is quite attraction enough for me," I respond, blushing at the same time, as I feel everybody knows I am going to see Amy.

"Blushing at eighteen, and a young man too—how absurd!" I fancy I hear somebody say.

Well, perhaps it is, but I could not help it, at that time, nevertheless.

"Ernest, my boy," says Uncle Joseph, "you have never told us how all the good folks at Edinburgh are, and what you have brought in that great hamper and box."

"Ah! I quite forgot; thinking so much of the pleasure of seeing you all again had quite driven out of my head all the messages."

"Has not Amy something to do with it?" whispers Ethel maliciously.

"Well, perhaps it has," thought I, but I didn't say so.

Next day we went to Anham. My sisters knew the way—I did not—and though I had some recollection of Miss Vernon's previsions about some old mansion I was to see, I was not prepared for so accurate a description as that she gave.

It was a lovely morning when we set out to walk to Anham Court, and it was the 24th of December—Amy's birthday. How I longed to present her something to show I loved—but I knew it would be resented if I, a mere boy, and with prospects so disproportionate to the de Courcy's standard of eligible young men, should so presume. I knew that in their eyes I should never be deemed worthy of their daughter's hand, and yet I *dared* to love her. What a lovely morning that was. and how happy we were, as we trudged along to see our friends at the old mansion! I was curious to see the place, and curious to see Amy, who had grown up since I had last seen her, and of whose memory, it must be owned, I was enamoured, rather than herself. As we entered the park, with its grand old elms, stately sycamores, and sturdy oaks lifting up their leafless branches to the skies, and swaying to and fro with melancholy sighing as the wintry winds whistled through them, I thought of the company of olden days that had been seen here. This old hall had belonged to the Lord of Valentra, and here in old time tournaments had been held. Knights, armed cap-a-pie in glittering steel, had tilted here before the noblest of the land; and once they bent their knee before King Edward III., when the king's grand-daughter had been wedded to Lord Aymer de Valentra. The snow had fallen, and was now frozen to the boughs of the trees, and covered the gables and roof of the old mansion. How cold it looked that day, and yet how pleasant. Christmas time seems always pleasant, even in an old deserted manor hall. The mansion itself was fast mouldering away, and the tapestries and ancient armour that hung within that hall have all disappeared. The old church was there, grey and somewhat gloomy, and the beautiful sloping lawn that went down to the river that passed beneath was covered with snow.

And there I saw Amy. I remember I hardly dared to look at her when she came into the room, and they all shook hands with us. And, when we went out into the garden for a stroll round before going home, I could not say a word, but only gazed upon her as she passed. Then I went back, scarce uttering a single word till we got home, and feeling that it was all over. I loved her without hope of winning her, and so I knew it would be till my dying day.

My brief visit to the south had done me good. I needed the change of air, and altogether I was not sorry I had seen Amy. I returned once more to Edinburgh and duty. I had hoped that my affection was for the ideal, and that when I should see her again I should find out that she was not *my ideal;* but, the moment I saw her I felt the reality, the force, and fervency of my passion for her, and, at the same time, felt the hopelessness of my suit. Every year I came down, at Christmas, to Gloucester, and every year contrived to see Amy. Eight winters had passed away—I was now twenty-six. Some changes had taken place in our family. One of my brothers had risen to be a lieutenant, and then fallen a sacrifice, in the Russian war, to the terrible ambition of a despot. The other was rising in the service. My sisters had all married, excepting the youngest, Ethel, who was as much my confidante as ever, and who knew that I was not going to marry anybody but one who lived in Gloucester, and if I could not marry her, I should live and die an old bachelor. I was young enough to change my mind; but she knew I would not do it. Mr. Vernon had removed to London, to carry on the better his researches into the genealogy of his family, and to assert his claims before the Committee of Privileges in the House of Lords. My eldest brother, Robert, had been from home several times since I had first known the Vernons; and, when opportunity offered, I gave him an introduction to them in London, and he used very often to go there to see them. He was on furlough, and came home in high spirits one day when he had just returned from London—whither he had gone, as he said, on special business—and told me he wanted to say something very particular if I could only come out for a walk.

How is it that we can talk better when rambling about?

"Well, Robert, and what is it all about?" I asked, as we were briskly walking out into the country on a fine frosty morning.

"You know, Ernest," he said, "how much I have seen of the Vernons for the last three or four years, and how much they have got to like me."

"Yes," I answered, "and what then, brother mine?"

"Oh, you stupid fellow," says Robert, "and can't you divine that I have fallen in love with the daughter, and she has accepted me."

"Oh, oh, is that it, my boy?" I responded, with something like a sigh; for I had flattered myself that Miss Vernon rather liked me, and, although I was in love with another, I suppose I should not have objected to think that the fair Annie was pining for me.

"Well, now that you have told me, Robert, I'll tell you what, I'm glad to hear it, and I heartily congratulate you, my dear boy, and if you had not got it you might have got something else—that's all," I remarked.

"What on earth do you mean, Ernest?" says Commander Robert—he was a commander now, in the Royal Navy.

"Why, just this. Do you remember my telling you about Mr. Vernon's claims for a peerage, which is dormant, and which he hopes to get called out of abeyance in his favour?"

"Yes. Well?"

"You know our mother was a Vernon, do you not?"

"Yes."

"Well, perhaps, you don't know that she was one of the heirs general to this title of Lord Vernon of Wye."

"No—is that so?"

"Yes. Since Mr. Vernon interested me in this subject I have, for the last five years, been poring over musty registers and old histories, and all sorts of curious documents, to arrive at the truth of the matter; and I think I have pretty well proved that all the descendants of the five sisters are dead, except Mr. Vernon's family and our own. If you had not been engaged to the young lady, I'm not so sure but I should have contested his claim to the title and estates. However, as, by your marriage with her, the two families are to be again united, all our claims are settled."

And so Robert made his confidences to me, and I told him about our pedigree.

It was another Christmas eve, and we were all down at Gloucester enjoying ourselves. Such a large party there was there. The De Courcy's had been invited to come; and the Vernons from London; and the two married sisters, with their husbands—one an artist, the other a physician; and a whole host of others. The Vernons could not come, as Mr. Vernon had been obliged to stay in London about this suit of his, which was expected to be settled definitively within a few days, and we were all rather anxious about it, more especially as every one now knew of Robert's engagement. I had been a little sad lately, for it was rumoured that Miss de Courcy was just engaged to a young officer, who had come to the barracks near the city; and I feared it was true, for he was well connected and sufficiently eligible. So I determined to ask her that night if this were so. It was New Year's Eve, and we had had a quite dinner, followed in the evening by a dance; and I had succeeded in engaging Miss de Courcy for a polka at the beginning of the evening. After the dance was over, instead of leading her to a seat and leaving her, I asked her to walk through the rooms with me, as I wanted to speak to her.

"Oh! certainly, I have no objection," she said, looking at me curiously.

Then we wandered through the rooms together, Miss de Courcy commenting on what she saw—sometimes kindly, sometimes satirically, as women will when they know what is coming—whilst I scarcely observed anything, but was thinking sadly how I should begin. It was a regular Christmas party, just such an one as my dear old uncle liked to gather round him on such an occasion. There were young people and married people, and old people, and little children, such a medley of our friends and such pleasant happy faces they seemed all to have. In one room we had contrived to settle down some of the elders; and as there were some notable whist players amongst them, the games did not lack in interest there. In another room we had packed most of the little ones away, where they were playing at "blind man's buff," and had just blindfolded Ethel as we entered the room. Ethel was very fond of children, and was a great favourite amongst the little ones. The carpet had been taken up in the large library leading from the hall, and here the dancing was going on. Little groups here and there were seen mostly in the corners and near the windows, who seemed to be engaged very pleasantly, especially where they were in couples. One or two disappointed maiden ladies, with imposing head-dresses and antique dresses, sat back, disgusted at the proceedings—especially such as still danced, or attempted to do so, and could not get partners for the next polka or quadrille. And there were a few wall-flowers scattered along the sides of the room; and the chivalrous gentlemen led these out to the dance, and did their duty well. And ever and anon my uncle's kindly face or my aunt's charming countenance beamed down upon them all; and then they went amongst the others—a pattern host and hostess. Then, at last, I mustered up courage, and determined to speak my whole mind once for whole.

"Miss de Courcy," I began, "do you remember that visit to Anham Hall, and how I could not speak to you?"

"Oh, yes, I remember. To tell you the truth, Mr. Blake, I thought you rather stupid."

How these words chilled me; but the decisive moment had come, and I must know my fate; so I just answered,

"Perhaps I was foolish then, and perhaps I am now; but it does not much matter. Will you let me take the privilege of an old friend, however, and congratulate you?"

"What about?" asks my fair friend, demurely.

"I heard that you were engaged to Captain Vesey. Is it true?" I asked carelessly, and yet waiting for an answer as if life or death depended upon it.

"Yes, it is perfectly true," she said, calmly.

"But what makes you so pale; and why do you startle?" she added.

"Oh! nothing—the heat of the room—a sudden spasm—it will be gone directly. There, I am well again, now. Here is Captain Vesey; let me hand you over to his care. *Au revoir.*"

I walked out into the cold air, and it refreshed me; and presently my sister Ethel came to me, and kissed me sorrowfully, but said nothing.

Ethel is coming to keep house for me now. I shall be an old bachelor; and so good bye, and happiness go with you all. The most momentous periods of our lives are oftentimes the shortest.

I should just add one line, to say that Mr. Vernon made good his claim to the peerage (chiefly through Miss Vernon's clairvoyant discoveries), and there were none to dispute it with him. He is now Lord Vernon, and his daughter the Hon. Mrs. Blake. Last Christmas-day a little boy was born, who is to be called Ernest Blake, and who will one day be Lord Vernon. Miss de Courcy married Captain Vesey, who was killed in the Indian mutiny, after having been made a major, and, through a cousin's death, coming in to the title of Lord Viscount Vesey, which he has left to a small boy, the very picture of his mother and not unlike his Lordship. Her Ladyship, the fair widow, who is still very young, has refused several offers since then; and I love her as much now as ever I did.

What will be the end of it? Who shall tell?

"ONLY A CHRISTMAS ROSE."

Far from the land where the mist o'er the river
   Settles in gloom on the sad winter day,
Where the cold winds made us cower and shiver,
   Thinking of sunny homes so far away,

Yon little maid and I caught in the northern blast,
   Hurried along where the waterfall throws
Myriads of rainbow tints, up in white vapour cast,
   Scattering foam blossoms, on its way goes.

What was it made me think, looking down on you then,
   Searching the depths of those dreamy brown eyes,
That life without you would ever be worthless, when
   With you such visions of joy could arise?

Ah! well I know not, but winter sounds pipe so loud;
   Cold beats the snow upon my little Rose,
Who, nestling close to me, with her head lowly bow'd,
   Happily homewards she on her way goes.

Out by the river side, out in the bleak north wind,
   Angel of mercy my bright one has been;
Taking some Christmas cheer to a lone sinner
   Who lives in the cottage away down the dene.

A poor stricken mortal, whom men had forsaken;
   A cast away thrown on a desolate shore;
Who, hopeless and faithless, by death was near taken,
   And lost in this world and the next evermore.

But my Rose had found him, one summer day's ramble,
   An old man and weary with life's heavy chain;

A past that was best forgot, future he heeded not,
    Present that was but one dreary with pain.

And she, the poor curate's fair only daughter,
    Pitied the trials and griefs of the poor;
And often she wander'd, and deeply she ponder'd,
    How to give help from her own little store.

Ah! well I bless the day which then sent me that way,
    Aimlessly roaming by sweet Orwell's side;
Only on pleasure bent, careless which path I went,
    Thinking of self whate'er might betide.

This little minist'ring angel who trod the path
    Of life and of duty in so pure a way,
Shamed me out myself, and thoughts of the aftermath
    Came to me, and shall stay by me alway.

My little Rose has made me think of others;
    Taught me that duty is now first of all;
How pleasure, like beauty, is fleeting, they're brothers,
    And to the true man they must ever soon pall.

Midst blushes that make her sweet face look far sweeter,
    She owns that one summer-tide not long ago,
She thought that some distant time—what could be sweeter?
    Fate might be propitious;—she loved me?—ah! no.

And I, well I'm free to own once when I saw her,
    Coming from church with her father one day,
I sketch'd the charming face, striving to catch the grace
    Of the bright winsome look that o'er it did play.

Well now she has promised some day that is far away,
    If I will wait for her, she will be mine;
But father is old, and him she must still obey,
    Till the death angel comes in his own time.

'Tis cold about us now out by the river
    Which widens its boundaries down to the sea;

ONLY A CHRISTMAS ROSE.

The storm birds are hovering hither and thither,
　But what are life's storms to her and to me?

I'll wait for her, live for her, strive to do bravely;
　Shield her from trouble, and give her repose;
I leave her at father's door, while she says gravely,
　And sadly, but sweetly, my little Rose:—

" Good bye, come and see me once more ere you leave us,
　Father will gladly your friendship accept,
And when you come again, oh, do not grieve us ":—
　My poor little maiden said no more, but wept.

A shadow, an icy blast, seem'd to pass by the porch;
　A nameless misery came like a dream,
And settled upon us both, as if death's flaming torch
　Had mark'd out a victim with its luried gleam.

" Good bye, my own darling," I said, and I kiss'd her,
　" A soldier's first word is duty, you know—
To-morrow my furlough is ended, but next year,
　Oh! many a walk by the river we'll go."

　　　*　　*　　*　　*　　*

Ah! I came back again to that sweet Orwell river
　A year or two after, perchance it was more;
I found that the cruel blasts of that harsh winter
　Had robb'd life of happy days for me in store.

There are flowers in heaven, I know, and I pray for
　The day that may take me where no winter snows
Shall ever more cover the grave of my lover;
　And I shall see once again my little Rose.

WAITING FOR HER.

A MESMERIST'S STORY.

CHAPTER I.

Uncle Archdale gave a Christmas party two years ago, and, of course, I was there. He is our bachelor uncle, you know. We have no parents, Lucy and I; but every Christmas day uncle had his nephews and nieces to dinner with him, and we always went with the rest. That year we went all together: not one of the family had left the nest; now, alas, they are all scattered, and perhaps may never meet again on this side of the grave.

Tom has gone to Australia. Philip has married my sister Lucy. He is a clergyman in the West Riding; and she makes a very good little parson's wife. My cousin Maud—dear Maud— has gone out as a governess, but some day I hope to be able to offer her a home. You see I live in a large town, and I am a young surgeon, without many friends; but I mean to push my way, and Maud is willing to wait—so I daresay we shall be married some fine day.

Bertie, and Mary, and Constance are with an uncle in Ireland; and Willie, poor boy, went to India and was drowned. Dear old Uncle Archdale died last year, he was then 60; and so I have told you how we were all separated.

Well, as I was saying, Uncle Archdale gave his usual Christmas party, and we were all there. I hardly know why he liked to give it either, for he was always rather grave on Christmas Day, though merry at other times; and, though he was kindness itself, yet on these occasions of our annual visit we always felt it rather melancholy dining at Alforde House.

After dinner we were sitting round the table at desert. There was a great fire burning in the grate, uncle had feasted us well, and we young fellows were very happy sipping our wine—some of the port was 1820 brand—whilst my fair cousins were more intent on the walnuts, almonds, and raisins, preserved ginger, ratafias and so forth, though of course they drank to a merry Christmas. Said Uncle Archdale—

"I think, my dears, I'll tell you a story."

"Oh, do, uncle," we all answered.

"Tell us about that pretty locket you always wear round your neck," Lucy slyly puts in.

I never saw the locket, but uncle seemed almost to wince as Lucy spoke.

"Tell us uncle," says Mary, "why you are always so grave on Christmas Day?"

"No, no, tell us," says Philip, "why you never got married?"

"Well, my dears," said my uncle, "suppose I answer you all three, and yet make one story of it?"

"Oh, do, uncle; we should like it so much," we all chorused.

"I don't know that you will care about the story, my dears," he said, "but perhaps it may do you no harm," he continued, looking particularly at Philip and me. I think he knew then all about our feelings, and about Lucy and Maud, for he smiled very kindly on them.

"It is a long time ago, my dears," he said, "since I first remember *waiting for her*, and I must wait a long time yet, I think, before she comes.

"You can look at her likeness if you like.

"Here it is;" and the old man—older in trouble and grief and care than in years—handed us out the locket containing the likeness of Millicent.

I have it now before me; he left it amongst other treasures to me in his will. What a sweet face it is! What soft, earnest blue eyes she has; what a placid, calm look of gentle innocence is there! She has her fair hair parted smoothly from her forehead, and looped up simply behind and fastened with some pretty comb, and she wears a little cross on her breast. And what a sweet oval, pensive face it is: the small, well-shaped mouth, the pure, serene brows, the smooth forehead, not so high as to make her look ugly and learned, nor yet so low as to be unintellectual. She must have had a graceful figure too, for, though we have but the head and bust here, we can see by the sloping shoulders, the well-set head and swan-like neck, that the harmony of nature *could not* be disturbed by giving a faulty figure to such a perfect face.

"It was Christmas time," my uncle continued, "in the year 1822, when I first saw Millicent, and at a Christmas party. I was only eighteen—and a mere boy—she was as old as I in years, and a great deal older in mind.

"Christmas Eve, and my father—your grandfather—(who was an artist, you know) had gathered the young people round him on this occasion, as was his wont, and a very jolly party it was. We used to romp more in those days, my dears, than you do now I fancy, and I think we loved each other more ardently than you do now. I dare say we fought more, too, and I don't suppose we were so refined altogether as the new generation is. However we had dancing, and hunt the slipper, and blind man's buff, and after supper kissing under the mistletoe.

"And I remember I kissed Millicent.

"I think I almost wish I had not done so now, for that kiss cost me a good deal; it cost me my heart, my dears."

"I don't know how it was, but so it was —from that hour to this I have loved Millicent.

"She didn't care for me, though," the old man continued. "She thought me a mere boy, and scorned my love. But what was that to me? I loved her, and I thought, foolish lad that I was, that if I were only constant to her, some day or other Milly would be mine; and so for years and years I was *waiting for her*."

"But did you never ask her to marry you?" Lucy asks.

"Oh, yes, my dear, I asked her, but I shall come to that presently.

"Well, it was before railways were thought of, and we were down in Somersetshire. We lived there then, and I was going up to town to walk the hospitals. I had come up from Exeter the night before, whither I had been sent by my father to see some creditors of his (he was an extravagant man, your grandfather, and always in debt), and who should get in at Bath but Millicent. She was also going to London to see her mother, who had been taken dangerously ill there. I had seen her many times since that Christmas party, and two years had gone over our heads. We had met frequently at various houses at Bath and Warminster, where she had relatives, and I had friends; and we were now pleasant acquaintance, if nothing more. So we journeyed on together; and, as you may imagine, I did not lose any opportunity to improve the occasion; and before we got to London I had asked her to be mine.

"Milly laughed outright at what she chose to call my effrontery in proposing to her, and 'such a boy as I was,' she said.

"Mortified, deeply wounded at her cruelty, so I thought then, I determined to leave the coach at the next stage, which was Reading, and leave Millicent and her aunt Frances to continue the journey by themselves.

"We soon reached Reading, and the coachman, whom I had

suspected of imbibing, got down to have just another glass at the hotel where we changed horses.

"It was a bitter cold night, on the 24th of December, 1824, when the Highflyer left the George and Dragon Hotel, at five p.m., for London. I was standing outside the door of the hotel, looking at the travellers with a pitying, self-satisfied air, as I thought how cold and uncomfortable they must be, and how cozy I should be when I went into the bar parlour and had a chat with mine host and his pretty daughter over a glass of his famous milk punch before the great blazing fire that was burning so pleasantly within.

"What was it made me order the hostler to get ready the light trap I had seen in the coach-house, just as they had gone, the four greys darting away with one bound as he lightly touched the off leader on the flank with his whip, and the guard blew his bugle merrily as they dashed off through the streets and out on the hard frozen high road on their way to the modern Babylon?

"Perhaps some presentiment of evil, unlooked for, unforseen. Perhaps only the fear arising from the very perceptible condition of the driver when he got on to his box and handled his ribbons.

"It was a quarter of an hour, however, before we started, and it would be only by hard driving that we could catch up the Highflyer—one of the fastest and most famous coaches of those days. I knew that about ten miles from Reading the high road turned an angle sharply over the low bridge which spanned a tributary of the Thames. The stream was wide here, and shallow enough to be easily forded in summer; but after the recent rains we had had, and the frost only now setting in, I knew the place to be a dangerous one, even to the most wary traveller, and doubly so when, as in the present case, it was very doubtful whether the bridge was not in an unsound state from the rottenness of the timbers of which it was principally composed:

and the condition of the coachman gave me also great uneasiness.

"'Now, my man, hurry on,' I said to the lad, half stable boy, half groom, who was driving me. 'I'll give you a crown if we catch them.'

"'All right, sir, we'll do it,' he answered.

"'Go it, Bess,' he continued to the horse—a young cob it was, I remember—touching her sharply over the shoulders with his whip. She answered with a bound, and set off at a fast trot, which, had it only continued, would have soon brought us up with the object of our anxiety. We were now three miles out of Reading, going at nine good miles the hour. The Highflyer did ten, but then she would probably stop at M———, a little village about eight miles from Reading, the lad said, as he heard the stout gentleman with the big cotton umbrella say he should get down there. He would persist in sitting outside with the guard, because, he said, 'He wasn't going to be boxed up with a parcel of women, though it was a cold night. Thank goodness he had enough of them at home without meeting his troubles halfway by seeking them elsewhere,' he gruffly, and not very politely, added.

"'And Mr. Markham,' that was the coachman's name. 'he'll stop at the Bag and Feathers, too, sir,' the lad continued; 'he always does stay for a toothful of "cold without" when he's had a drop, sir. If you don't mind, sir,' the boy said presently, 'we'll just cut across the common here, sir. It's rather dark, but I know every inch of the way, and it'll save us a good three miles, sir, every bit of it.'

"'All right, my lad,' I said, 'only catch the coach before she passes Hammon's corner (the place I have alluded to) and I'll give you another crown.'

"Away we went over the common: it was now pitch dark—a

cloudy sky and the snow slightly falling. Across the smooth and hardened turf, at full gallop—away we went for life and death Presently we heard the sound of wheels, distant at first, but growing painfully nearer every moment. Oh, if they should pass the corner before we were there! If the huge coach, guided by the drunken brute who now held the reins (but who was only overtaken at Christmas time, and famed as the best whip in the three counties, as his apologists averred) should swerve but a few inches from the path, it and its precious cargo would be submerged in the now rapid rushing stream, Milly, my own Milly, would be drowned before my eyes. The thought maddened me.

"Lashing the horse furiously, we dashed forward at renewed speed, and crossed the bridge just before the mail coach came up. Markham was driving viciously; one moment more and we should have been too late.

"The leader, frightened at the white coping stones of the bridge covered with snow, and wild with the treatment he had evidently received, now suddenly turned, was rushing across the road, making as it were for the parapet of the bridge, and in a moment the coach which had been swaying to and fro was dragged forward towards the stream, into which it would have fallen had not I drawn up across the road, jumped out of the trap, seized the leader, and forced him back almost on his haunches, till I had driven back the coach, which had received a check from coming into contact with the large curb-stone at the corner of the bridge, into the road again. Another dash made by the off horse —another swerving of the coach, and she was thrown violently over on her side, and two of the horses fell to the ground. 'Here, lad, here; not a moment to spare,' I shouted to the boy; and by great exertions we broke open the door, and helped the ladies out. Poor things! they were both hurt seriously, though not so seriously as I had feared. The coach was almost smashed to atoms, and the coachman lay with his leg broken at some distance from the vehicle. The horses were soon disengaged from the harness, and the old gentleman, who, wonderful to say, had got off with only a few bruises, rode off, on one of them, in search of a doctor.

"I determined to take the ladies back with me to Reading, leaving the guard, who was himself almost uninjured, to attend to the coachman and the horses.

"Poor Milly! how brave she was. I helped her up very tenderly, you may be sure; her arm was broken, but she bore the pain so quietly, bidding me only look after Aunt Frances, who was very much terrified, and whose nerves appeared to have been terribly shaken by the unfortunate mishap, but who was otherwise uninjured as far as I could learn.

"'Madge,' she said presently, 'will you forgive me behaving so unkindly to you as I did to-day. I am very grateful to you for coming to our assistance when you did. I feel somehow as if I owed my life to you, and you can do with me what you like now.'

"'Thank you, dear,' I said quietly, 'I shall always love you;' that was all the answer I made.

"We got back to Reading, and as we had no friends there, the ladies stopped at the George and Dragon, and I determined to stay by them, until some one should come to take charge of them, or they should be able to go on to London.

"You see we had no telegraph then, and no express trains, to let our friends know in an hour or two after the accident what had happened, or to bring them to us as soon as now.

"It would take two days at least to bring our friends from Bath, and a whole day or more to get to London. So I remained where I was, simply writing down to my father and to Milly's to tell what had happened. The few days that followed, my dears, were the happiest days of my life, I think. Aunt Frances—I used to call her so, though she was no actual relation of my mother's—was very poorly the next day, and poor Milly was quite feverish and low; but yet she would not obey the doctor's directions to stay in bed after the second day, but would come down stairs in the parlour (I had taken private rooms for the party) and talk to me. Oh, how I drank in the music of her voice! How I listened, and looked, and loved! I knew she was grateful to me for *saving her life*, she said—though I don't know that I did that exactly—and I felt that she was mistaking that sentiment for love; and she thought then that she might *some day*, that she did *then*, return my affection.

"She was so kind and gentle to me in those days, and never was slave more willing than I to wait upon her and obey her behests. It was one long golden dream. I knew it could not last. I knew the spell would be broken soon. I knew that in a few days, perhaps a week at the farthest, her mother, who we had heard was getting better, would send some one for her, and I knew that when that some one came I must be gone.

"The arm was obstinate, or surgeon unskilful, and what should have taken only a fortnight or so, took a month or more.

"And as the days wore on we became more and more to each other. Milly was becoming all the world to me, and I was ceasing to be merely a pleasant passing acquaintance in her eyes, but a warm admiring friend.

"Sometimes I used to fancy that she loved me, but I soon found the love was only gratitude.

"I think at that time, my dears, Milly would have married me; but I knew it would not have been for love and love only, and I scorned to take her simply for gratitude's sake.

"Was I right, I wonder, in going away as I did without saying another word?

"I don't know, I only know that she was my heart's one idol, and I was *waiting for her.*"

CHAPTER II.

WE were still sitting round the fire. Philip had just put a great log of wood on, and Lucy was saying that it was far too pleasant to have the lights brought in yet, it was so cosy sitting in the firelight listening to uncle's story.

"Take another glass of wine, uncle," Tom said, "you will be getting tired of talking."

"Well, I think I will, my boy," Uncle Archdale replied, rousing himself.

He had been looking dreamily into the fire for the last ten minutes, and had never spoken a word.

"Now, boys, you must look after yourselves," he said, cheerily; "remember this is Liberty Hall! Tom, I think the bottle is with you.

"And you, young ladies, I suppose you would like to go up to the drawing room and have some music?"

"Oh, please, uncle, we would much rather stay here and listen to your story; let Mary bring in the coffee here," Lucy put in. She was the oldest, and, therefore, fit spokesman—woman, I should say.

"As you please, young people," he answered, "as you please."

So we had tea down stairs, and Aunt Miriam rang the bell, and gave the desired order.

Aunt Miriam was Uncle Archdale's eldest sister, who kept house for him. A very quiet old maid, with whom we did just as we liked. She was a *maiden lady*, I should say, not an *old maid*; the distinction is obvious. I know many a dear old maiden lady with no queer ways, no cold-hearted whims and oddities, no desire to snub young people and back-bite their neighbours, but women with warm young hearts and generous sympathies: always trying to do their best to win the love of all around them by their deeds of beneficence and charity, and trying to merit also the approbation of the Almighty Disposer of us all. I did not mean to digress in this way, but I can't bear to hear people carping at single ladies for being single.

Dear me, I know many a one single from choice; and let me tell you, young people, it's my belief that there are very few women indeed but have had chances of marrying if they liked.

"Well, my dears," uncle began, "I suppose you wish me to go on with my story?"

"Yes, yes," we all answered.

"Imagine then, my dears," uncle went on, "that two years had passed away. I was entered at St. Thomas' Hospital. Dr. Elliotson was then Assistant Physician there: he had been elected to that post in 1817. It was not till 1837 that he owned himself the leader of the mesmeric party; but at this time, 1824, mesmerism was much discussed amongst the students at St. Thomas; and about three years later, Professor Gregory, who had filled the chair of Chemistry at Edinburgh, had his attention drawn to the subject by Monsieur Comdet, of Geneva, who had seen the famous cases of Dr. Petetin, of Lyons, whose work on the subject I read.

"I had become much interested in the subject, and had determined, if opportunity should offer, to try for myself the truth or falsehood of mesmerism.

"An opportunity did offer, and sooner than I expected. But I must not anticipate. Since the day when I gave up the charge of Millicent I had never seen her but twice. She had gone home, had speedily recovered, and the last tidings I had heard of her were, that she was engaged to be married to a young clergyman, who had recently come to reside in the neighbourhood of Orley House, Mr. Bertram's residence.

"Mr. Bertram, Milly's father, was a gentleman of great pride and of undoubted family. The Barony of Bertram, of which he was one of the claimants, had fallen into abeyance in 1311, when Roger, son and heir of the first Baron (so created 1264) died, leaving an only daughter. Agnes, who, dying s. p., as the heralds say, the Barony fell into abeyance amongst the descendants of her four aunts, daughters of the first lord. I merely mention this to show that if he was proud of his family and lineage, length and nobility of descent were some excuse.

"He owned a small estate in the country, and had contracted but few intimacies amongst his neighbours, except your grandfather, who had been one of the notable exceptions.

"I don't think I ought to blame Milly for changing so suddenly. She had not indeed changed really, only she had fancied she loved me, and now she found she did not. Looking back upon it now I *cannot* blame her. I had now been some two years in London, and had never written to her, as indeed I had no right to do; but though my sister had seen her often, she never sent a kindly message to me—perhaps fearful to give me encouragement—and I, equally proud with herself, never expressed any desire to know how or where she was. I knew she *liked* me, but I knew she did not *love* me, so I had been waiting for a sign of the change, and lo! this was the sign:

"—the idol of my heart—the one hope of my life—she to whom I had secretly and sacredly affianced myself, as I madly thought, though she had never been a party to the bargain, poor girl—she whom I so fervently, passionately, and deeply loved—had bestowed the whole wealth of her affections upon another, and I—I—was left alone.

"What would I not give to make her love me! What would I not do to make her wholly mine! A sudden thought came over me and made me shudder as I pictured it in my mind.

"What was this new science of mesmerism—this wonderful power of fascination? Could it be used to make her bow to my will—could I make her yield to my wishes?

"I should tell you that I lodged in London with one Mrs. Wingrove. Ralph Wingrove, who was a distant connection of her husband's, and who was my chum at St. Thomas', first took me there, and I soon changed my quarters to come and live with the family at Bloomsbury. Kate Wingrove was a sweet, nice girl, very lady-lake, with black ringlets and a pale face. They were, I'm afraid, what Mr. Thackeray would call a shabby-genteel family—indeed Mrs. Wingrove was a decayed gentlewoman, who was forced to make a living out of her boarders. I rather think they fancied I wanted Kate. We certainly were great friends, and I was very much interested in her, poor girl—for there was something indescribably mysterious that attracted us to each other, and made us seek each other's society far oftener than perhaps was good for either. Mrs. Wingrove trusted Kate and trusted me so thoroughly, however, that there was no bounds to our intimacy.

"I think in this she was wrong, as the sequel will show.

"Ralph and I were tyros in mesmerism.

"One day he said to me, 'I say, Madge, did it never strike you that Kate would make a good *clairvoyante?* I think that's the new name for these extatic mesmeric subjects?'

"'Well, I will confess the idea has entered my mind,' I said.

"'Why not try her?' he went on.

"'I don't know, I'm sure; perhaps she would object.'"

"'Not a bit of it, old fellow—not at *your* hands, I'll promise you.'

"'Well, some day we'll try the experiment, if Kate's agreeable.'

"Singular to say, that very night Kate was complaining of neuralgia in the face and head.

"I offered to try and cure her, and thus began our mesmeric seances.

"Would to God they had ended there.

"In ten minutes I had succeeded in putting her into a profound sleep. Mrs. Wingrove and Ralph both present. In five minutes more I required her to awake refreshed and recovered.

"And she did so.

"Charmed with my success, we were led to make further experiments, and I soon found that Kate possessed the true *clairvoyante* faculty. The study of animal magnetism is a strangely fascinating one; and within six months I had so completely gained possession of Kate's will, that I could send her into a profound slumber in the course of a minute or two. I remember one night, when she had gone off into a state of *coma*, and I was asking her questions relating to all things from time unto eternity, she suddenly startled me by saying—

"'I see a fair lady, with such a sweet, sad, pensive face,' she added; and in a minute she continued, 'it is the same face as that in your locket.'

"'Where is she?' I asked.

"'I cannot tell.'

"'But you must,' I replied—and I touched her heaving bosom, her eyes, and her lips, with a little magnetised steel rod, which I carried about with me—at the same time placing in her hand the locket containing Millicent's likeness and a lock of her beautiful hair.

"My good sister Miriam got me this a year or two ago, and I

always wore it next my heart. Milly did not even dream of its existence.

"In a minute or two, with a deep-drawn sigh, she said,

"'I see, now. She is standing in a garden which crowns a lofty hill—a pretty house built like an Elizabethan cottage is behind her—in the distance is a wide spreading landscape with great hills on either side—and the river running between them. She is talking with a gentleman.'

"'What is he like?' I asked.

"'Well, he is tall and slight, with auburn hair, and large eyes. He is pale and rather sickly looking—and looks like a clergyman.'

"'My rival,' I thought.

"'Yes, your rival.' *She answered to my thought.* I started. Has it come to this, I said to myself, that one can even read another's thoughts.

"'Kate,' I said, do you think you can impress Millicent with the thought that I love her?'

"'I will try,' she said. 'but you must will it too with all your own power.'

"Presently a smile crept over her face, and she said softly,

"'It is done! I see her start, and then grow sad and thoughful. She is thinking now. She wishes she could love you.'

"'Is there any hope?'

"'Yes,' she said fervently, after a long pause, 'yes, if——'

"'If what,' I urge impatiently.

"'If your rival were out of the way.'

"'Out of the way,' I muttered to myself, 'out of the way.'

"A horrid thought seized me.

"'Can you impress him?' I muttered fiercely.

"'For your sake I will try.'

"For my sake. What was this? I paused to collect my thoughts. I let her rest awhile whilst I think. That last effort

of hers did her harm, I fancy, for she put her hand to her side
and complained of her heart beating so fast and feebly.

"She had said to me once, 'You can do anything with me; I
am powerless in your hands; you will kill me some day.'

"'Do impress him, then, from me. *Haunt* him,' I said
sternly. 'Let him think this of Millicent. *She shall be mine,
not his.*'

"'Take my hand, press it hard,' Kate said, 'and send your
will with it.'

"I did so; she remained quiet for a minute, and then half
rose from the sofa on which she was reclining, heaved a deep sigh,
and fell back apparently utterly prostrated.

"'Wake me,' she said, 'Wake me, I am in pain!'

"I got up for a moment, slowly made the passes over her, and
firmly replied these words—

"'Be calm and be refreshed.'

"In a few minutes she recovered: but again begged me to
awake her.

"'Did you affect him?' I ask.

"'Yes.'

"'How?'

"'When you pressed my hand, I went to him, and I impressed
him with your thought.'

"'What did he do?'

"'He fell to the ground.'

"'What then?'

"'I could see no further.'

"I mused awhile. 'Kate,' I said, at length, 'I want to talk
to you. Sleep for an hour,' I continued; 'sleep and be refreshed.'

"I waved my hands slowly over her for a few minutes, until
she sank into a sleep so profound as would have startled the neo-
phyte magnetist; but I knew that she would derive fresh vigour

and support from so peaceful a slumber; and she would be of service to me in my schemes when she recovered. Kate's was a dual existence now. I was sapping her very life's blood to attain my own selfish end; but what did I care for that? I loved Millicent, and I had determined she should be mine. Circumstances had been against me of late.

"Mrs. Bertram, even before Milly was engaged to Mr. Thornton, had discovered my secret, and had discouraged my visits to the house in consequence.

"I had not yet got my certificates from the College of Surgeons, so was not in anything like a position to marry. Had I been so, I should have tried my fortunes once again, and faced a second refusal from her lips; but it was useless going to her now when I had nothing to offer.

"I had thought the Bertrams were mercenary, but it was clear they were not so, or they would not have allowed their daughter to be engaged to so poor a man as this Mr. Thornton must be. If I could only drive him away—I did not wish to do him harm—perhaps she might get to like me.

"'In love and war all politics are fair,' I said to myself. 'I don't suppose it will harm him.'

"In an hour exactly Kate awoke;—that is to say, she came out of the deathlike trance in which she had been lying, into the usual lucid state in which she was previously.

"I should tell you, that when Kate was awake to self-consciousness she liked me, that was all. When she was under the influence of my magnetic power she loved me—she was my slave.

"It is an awful power for one human being to have over another.

"Mesmerism is like other of God's good gifts—it can be perverted to evil.

"'Kate,' I said, 'I want you to help me. Will you do so?'

"'Yes.'

"'Whatever I ask you to do?'

"'Yes,' she answered slowly, almost sorrowfully, 'whatever you command I must obey.'

"'Then I wish to marry Millicent.'

"'Do you?' she murmured, with a sigh.

"'Yes, and you can help me to win her, by removing all obstacles from my path. Look for the clergyman; do you see him?'

"After a long while she murmured painfully,

"'No, I cannot find him.'

"I touched her with the rod of steel. She bounded as if a flame of fire had darted through her, and then replied, faintly,

"'I see him.'

"'Where?' I ask.

"'In the house; he is reclining on the sofa, and they are all round him.'

"'What is he saying?'

"'He is telling them that he had a horrid dream, that was all. That some one came behind him, and pressed his hand so painfully that he turned round, but no one was there, and he heard words like this: "Millicent! she shall be mine, not thine!"'

"I smiled at this triumphantly, and then I formed a resolution.

"'Kate, you can wake now,' I said, and she awoke.

"I resolved then in my own mind that I would haunt him."

CHAPTER III.

Tea had been brought in, and taken out again, before Uncle Archdale continued his story. He had left the room just before tea, and had returned from the surgery with a packet of letters or papers evidently taken from the *escritoire*.

Uncle did not practice now. He had acquired a little property, and some great aunts of ours had left him money, and he was very comfortably off; only he would persist in calling his library the surgery, though there was not a bottle or potion in it.

"Well," my uncle said, as he sat down again, "I suppose, my dears, I must finish my story."

"Oh, yes, if you please, we should like to hear the end, and we are not at all tired," Lucy replied.

"Well, then, I will tell you the rest," he continued.

"The usual time for walking the hospitals had passed away, it was three years then—now I think it is five," my uncle resumed.

"I had just got my certificates from the Apothecaries' Company and College of Surgeons, testifying to my efficiency in compounding nasty medicines, and in setting compound fractures, and so forth.

"Medicine was nasty in those days; now they make it pleasant to the taste, don't they, young man?" he said, turning to me.

"Well sir, we have improved a little in that way, I believe."

"Yes," uncle continued, "I had come out a full blown surgeon and general practitioner; I had left the Wingroves, very much to Kate's grief, and her mother's dismay. The latter had quite made up her mind I should marry her daughter, though Kate, poor girl, knew well enough who it was I was waiting for. The extraordinary power I had exercised over her had increased with time, and by means of her *clairvoyant* dreams, I had kept myself informed of Millicent's whereabouts. From my sister, too, I learned occasionally what was going on, though she seldom saw the Bertrams now, as my father had left the neighbourhood, and gone to live at Salisbury. This much I knew, however, that Milly was still unmarried, and Mr. Thornton was still constant to her.

"I should tell you that the night before I left Bloomsbury—it was the 6th of October, 1827—I had a long *seance* with Kate: it might be the last I should ever have, and I felt that now or never I must act. As you may scarcely credit the story, Lucy shall read you this letter about it," and he handed to her an old franked letter, yellow with age, and dusty, written in a weak, feeble hand, the hand of a sick man. There was an endorsement on the back, which ran thus:—

"This letter from Edmund Thornton given to me by Millicent Bertram on Christmas morning, 1830."

"Thretford Parsonage, 7th October, 1827.
"MY DEAREST,—
"I don't know how to write this letter.
"I am afraid you will think me mad.
"I am afraid I am mad. Forgive me if I am incoherent; but so much has troubled me of late, that I think sometimes I am tried more than other men. I have a fearful presentiment that we *shall* never—that we *can* never—be married. Sometimes these warnings come to me more palpably than at other times. Sometimes when I am sitting in my study reading of an evening, I feel a pressure on my arm, and I turn and see by my side a figure, that of a lady, with a pale face and long black elf locks,

and a voice seems to come from afar off, saying, 'Millicent shall be mine, never thine.' Not once or twice only have I seen this, but many times. It is killing me. No man can be braver than I can be, where any earthly material danger exists, but this perpetual haunting of a spiritual presence threatens to turn my brain.

"The horrors of last night, if they should return, will deprive me of my reason.

"I feel it going even now. I have prayed against it, but God has not seen fit to hear my prayer. Perhaps it is sent to try me. I know not, but this I know, that in life or in death, I strive to serve Him. And I love you, oh my darling, as I shall ever love you, purely, devotedly, and constantly.

"Last night I had retired early to my room, for I had been suffering from a severe cold. It was about ten o'clock, and I was sitting for a few minutes over the fire in my bed-room musing, when suddenly I felt a hand, a woman's hand, grasp my arm. I turned, and saw as plain as eye could see, a tall woman by my side. It was the pale lady with the black ringlets. She frowned upon me, and I shuddered as I saw another hand steal out of the space, holding a wand of fire.* In the wand seemed to lay the mysterious influence which paralysed me.

"I shall never forget that hand. Upon one finger was a ring formed like a serpent, with its tail in its mouth, and its eyes were jewels. Out of the space came a voice, the same voice I had heard before, and it said—*Millicent shall be mine, never thine!* At the sound of these words I fell to the ground, and when I next became conscious, I found I had been put into bed, and the

---

* SENSITIVES can perceive magnets in the dark by the light they emit. Mesmeric subjects often describe flames of light issuing from the tips of fingers, and from the eyes of the operator. A magnetised rod would appear to be illuminated to a SENSITIVE. The reader is referred to Reichenbach's Researches in Magnetism, for further information on this subject.

doctor had come to see me, as the landlady had sent word that I had taken a fit.

"Oh, that horrible night, the remembrance of it is so appalling that I am seized with fearful pain about the heart whenever I think about it, and a violent trembling comes upon me. * * *

"I left off there because the doctor came, and now he says I am suffering from an affection of the heart, and any great excitement would be dangerous. I am to go away from here, as the air, he says, appears to have an enervating effect upon me.

"Of course it is no use speaking to him of what I saw.

"Dearest, dearest Milly, I hope nothing may come to separate us. God bless you, my own.—Your ever loving,

"EDMUND."

Maud looked up when Lucy had finished reading this letter, and said—

"Uncle, you have a ring like a serpent on your finger, and it has diamonds for eyes."

"Yes, my dear, I have," my uncle answered—nothing more.

"To resume then.

"In three months from that date I was settled at H., about half way between Warminster and Salisbury. One of my aunts had advanced £1,000 to place me with me the medical man of that place as his partner. I went up to London once, to spend a day or two with some friends, and stayed two evenings with the Wingroves.

"Kate was glad to see me, you may be sure, so was Mrs. Wingrove.

"The last evening I was there I sent Kate to *haunt* Mr. Thornton.

"She described the scene.

"'Where is he?' I asked.

"'He is with a lady,' she answered, 'the same lady I saw

before. I think he has come to spend Christmas with them. They are sitting in the drawing room. She has been singing to him; and he to her. The last song he sung was, "When other lips," I think, for I see it on the top of some music on the piano. Now she is leaving the room. She has gone away for something. He is sitting over the fire. How pale and wan he looks."

"'*Impress him from me!*' I said.

"'Oh, no, do not harm him any more; you will kill him.

"'I care not what I do,' I said, 'has he not robbed me of my heart's idol? Go to him,' I continued sternly.

"'Oh! do not force me,' she said, pleadingly, 'you have injured him enough. See what a wreck he is already!'

"'It is enough,' I angrily rejoined. 'Obey me.'

"She fell back upon the sofa on which she had been reclining, and swooned away.

"I heeded her not, but paced the room for some minutes; then I approached her where she lay, placed my hands upon her shoulders, breathed upon her cold brows, and in a few moments she had recovered.

"'Wake me,' she said, 'oh, wake me; I am in pain.'

"'Tell me,' I asked, 'where is he?'

"'I cannot see him.'

"'Look,' I said, and I touched her again with my steel rod.

"'Ah!' she answered, with a sigh of pain and anguish.

"'What is it?' I asked.

"She burst into tears, and in a moment would have been in hysterics, had I not again placed my hands upon her shoulders, and breathed upon her calmness and repose.

"'Answer me, what is the matter?'

"I shall never forget the feeling that came over me, when she replied, slowly, and with awful solemnity,

"'*He is dead, and you have killed him.*'

"The jury brought in a verdict of 'Died by the visitation of God.'

"Ah, my dears," the old man said, "never let passion get the mastery over you; never try to accomplish your ends, whatever they may be, by foul means. Had I never heard anything of mesmerism, I should have been a happier man; but I have repented now of my wickedness, and I trust I am forgiven."

The old man was affected by the memory of the past, and I saw him clasp his hands as if in prayer for a moment or two, and then he bowed his head.

"Why did you not marry Millicent after all, uncle?" Maud presently asked.

"There, my dear, is the saddest part of the story. I was overcome with remorse, and never could bear to hear the subject of mesmerism mentioned since. Of course I had not meant to kill poor Edmund—all I wanted to accomplish was his retirement or dismissal. I wanted to frighten him into the belief that his marrying Millicent was impossible, and that if ever it were possible it would prove fatal to her happiness and to his; but I never dreamed of the dreadful ending of my plot, and the reaction upon myself was frightful. I was taken severely ill. For weeks I lay at death's door; and months had passed away before I had recovered. I was a changed man;—changed in everything, save my undying love for Millicent.

"Before Edmund's death I had been a man careless about religion, but now I was a poor penitent sinner, humbly trying to lead a new life, to fit me for that eternity to which we are all hurrying."

The old man spoke reverently, and his solemn words made a deep impression upon us.

"And, my dears, I was still waiting for Milly.

"Two years passed by.

"Time, the great restorer, had done much to soften her grief, but her sorrows had been a great trial to her, and she bore it well. The darling, I see her now. Her face had grown more pensive—the cheek had lost its bloom; the smile had grown more sweet, and the laugh was still as silvery as ever, only we did not hear it often now.

"She knew I loved her, but she could not bring herself to think of me as anything but a friend—a brother.

"She knew nothing of my *magnetic hauntings*—nothing of my mesmeric seances.

"Poor Edmund had died of heart disease—they all knew that; he had suffered from it long, and then he had been subject to epileptic fits.

"She always knew he was delicate.

"I was now getting into a good country practice, and could offer Milly a home, but I did not like to hurry her.

"Another Christmas party at Warminster, and Milly was invited.

"Mr. Wybrants was the medical man with whom I had served my apprenticeship, and he gave a large annual party.

"I had never been before, but this year I had resolved to go, if only to meet Milly, who was staying with an aunt there, and who knew I had accepted the invitation.

"I had made up my mind to give her another invitation. Would she accept mine?

"It was a merry party; young people, and old people, and middle-aged people, and children were there, and it was Christmas Eve.

"How I love the little Children!—I should have liked to have had some of my own, but Providence has seen fit that it should be otherwise.

"I had not enjoyed it so much as I had expected: I had

romped enough with the children it is true. We had blind man's buff, and they made me a blind man.

"Then we had snapdragon, and I burned my fingers, getting out the raisins for little Lizzie, and Girtie, and Alice.

"And after the children had gone we had dancing, and I kissed dear old Mrs. Wybrants under the mistletoe. How they did all laugh! 'Just like the old bachelor,' they said.

"And we had a nice supper, too, and good port and sherry to wash it down—none of your nasty French wines. Champagne was very dear then, and one seldom tasted it in the country, except at the Hall, perhaps, or at the Court. But I did not much enjoy it, for Millicent was not there.

"The doctor gave me a bed, and, feeling tired with my exertions, and with romping with the children, I retired early. Mrs. W. had told me casually, in reply to my inquiries about Milly, that she was afraid she was very poorly, but she hoped there was no danger.

"*Very poorly, no danger,* I muttered to myself. I never knew she was unwell.

"It was too late to call at the house, and ask after her. My presence would only disturb her perhaps; and then I thought remorsefully how happy I had been playing with the children all the while she was ill. So I determined to go the first thing in the morning: and comforting myself with that thought I fell asleep.

"I must have slept for two hours or more; when I awoke, the clock was striking one. It was a lovely winter moonlight night, and I could see out of the window the snow thick upon the gables opposite ours. It was very cold—bitterly cold. What was that icy blast that passed me there? I looked up—and saw —Milly standing at the foot of my bed, and the rays of the moon shone upon her, but her *figure threw no shadow on the floor.*

"I was not frightened, but an inexpressible grief came over me

—a feeling of utter desolation was upon me. I gazed with awe, but with no craven fear upon the form—and then it slowly vanished from my eyes. My dears, I got up, and I fell upon my knees at the foot of my bed, and I prayed the Almighty to spare her to me. I prayed that this might not be a foreshadowing of the end—and then afterwards I slept.

"In the morning I found that letter in my room, which Lucy has read to you. In the morning I heard that which sent the blood back ice cold to my heart—I heard that Millicent had died at one o'clock on Christmas morning.

"So you see, my dears, that is the story of the locket—that is the reason I have never married—that is the reason I am always sad on Christmas day. I had loved her many years—I had done wrong to try and win her. I had repented, but I was punished for my sin. I was waiting for her then—I am waiting for her now—waiting for the great day of account, when I may claim her again perhaps—waiting till then!"

The old man ceased—the tears were standing in his eyes. He slowly got up and left the room, and we saw him no more that night. Poor uncle! his heart was so full that he could not even wish us good night, and so was forced to leave us, lest we should see the weakness of tears.

THE END.

A STRICKEN HEART.

In every bush the sweet birds sing,
   On every bough the buds have come;
All nature speaks of balmy Spring,
   Of resurrection from the tomb.

The scented May on every hedge,
   The cuckoo calling to his mate;
A gladsome look is everywhere,
   And only I am desolate.

A world of happiness around;
   The picture of a fair young life;
So full of hope, and peace, and love,
   As though there were no fear or strife.

I stood at brink of mossy dell,
   And listen'd to the warblers there;
And wonder'd at sweet Philomel,
   As loud he chanted to his fair.

Why sing the birds on every tree?
   Why glow the fields with bright wild flowers?
What all this vernal wealth to me,
   Who nevermore have happy hours?

Be still, sad heart, no more repine;
   Should all the world be sad for thee;
What, if the brightness of thy life
   Have gone, and joy no more can be?

The earth is fair; some hearts are kind;
   And nature now how glad she seems;

The young lambs gambol in their joy,
　　The morning sun hath rosy beams.

The verdant meads are wet with dew,
　　The modest violet hangs her head
In mossy brake, where daffodils
　　Have bloom'd on saffron-tinted bed.

Take heart of grace, and look on these,
　　And thank the Maker of them all,
That he hath made a world so bright,
　　And granted joy to great and small.

Doth Death come only now to thee?
　　Hath Love betray'd no other one?
Ah, tear-drops fall from other eyes,
　　And gloom comes when the day is done.

The grey clouds sail across the sky,
　　And cast deep shadows o'er the meads;
There is no joy for cloister'd nun,
　　Nor grey-clad friar who tells his beads.

The fire of life hath long gone out,
　　The glow of love long quench'd hath been;
And only the cold grey of life,
　　Remains for these; no more is seen.

Yet they are well content, and thou
　　Must learn to be resign'd as they,
Remembering that, though Spring-time now,
　　The autumn is not far away.

With patient waiting peace will come,
　　And grace to bear thy weary load;
So pray that when thy earthly home
　　Thou leavest for that bright abode—

In those celestial mansions where
　　An everlasting Spring-time reigns,

A STRICKEN HEART.

And there shall be no Summer glare,
   Nor melancholy Autumn strains;

No winds that sigh through empty aisles,
   Of leafless trees in forest vast;
Thou wilt remember, yet forget,
   The pain of life which now is past.

So welcome Autumn's slow decay,
   And welcome death and Winter's pall,
When "flowers are in their grassy tombs,
   And tears of dew are on them all." *

---

* This exquisite thought is from Hood's Poem on Autumn.

HOPELESSLY;

OR, MADGE RAYMOND'S MIDNIGHT RIDE, AND WHAT CAME OF IT.

CHAPTER I.

INTRODUCTORY.

ON the Christmas Eve in the year of grace 1859, the good town of Marton-on-the-Hill was very gay; all the shops were open till a late hour, and numbers of pedestrians, principally of the "lower orders," might be seen wending their way to the High-street, to buy their Christmas dinner. It had been snowing heavily, and the night was sharp and frosty. Very pretty looked the old town that night; and very happy looked the faces of the people as they crowded in and out the shops. These latter were gaily decorated with evergreens, and wonderful devices in fruit and vegetables, tricked out with coloured papers of astonishing and curious patterns.

I don't know that an artist would say much for the taste displayed in these preparations for the festivities of Christmas; but the motto in almonds, on a bed of raisins, "A Merry Christmas to You;" or, "A Happy New Year," done in oranges, upon a lovely background of currants, spoke to the warm hearts of the work people in a language significant of Christmas cheer, and elicited from them warmer expressions of approbation, probably, than anything more artistic might have produced.

Marton had been the centre of an agricultural district until the last few years, and nothing more. It had its cattle show and fair once a year—the show held late in December, the fair in August. Generally, too, they managed to get up a Hunt Dinner and Ball during Christmas week. Otherwise, it had been rather a dull place to live in; and the youth of Marton had had a hard time of it to get anything like rational amusement after office hours. Extensive potteries and ironworks had, however, been recently opened, and Marton had begun to taste of the prosperity which had come upon its sister towns in Staffordshire. Situated within 150 miles of town, and with the new branch lines to Macclesfield and Newcastle-under-Lyme just completed, easy communication was opened to the great towns in the neighbourhood, and trade was springing up again.

But there had been a strike in the Iron Trade, the staple business of the town. There had been also one or two failures in the other great branches of commerce, and much distress had prevailed.

Marton, however, was, as I said before, an agricultural as well as a manufacturing town. The harvest this year had been good, and the fair just passed had been the best attended for many a year past. The strike was now over, and the men had come to an agreement with the ironmasters, which, as it was likely to be profitable to both, promised to be more satisfactory than any of the previous overtures which had been made on either side. The great firms which had collapsed, had given place to new companies, formed upon surer bases, with men of integrity, talent, energy, and capital to back them, at their head; and Marton once more looked up.

No wonder, then, that the poor people looked happier this Christmas time. Many an one could go to church to-morrow, who had not been there this long time, to thank God for His present mercies to them, and to pray hopefully for a blessing upon them in the future.

The old church stands in the centre of the town, but surrounded by a large grave-yard, now long disused. Some fine elm trees overshadow it: they make a famous rookery in summer time; but the birds have deserted it now. Marton smoke has not yet killed them; but ere long, no doubt, 'twill do its work, and the last remnant of the country in the heart of Marton will die its death.

Let us step inside the church. It is lighted up we see—not for service though. They are putting the last touches to the decorations; and pretty Miss Birch, the Vicar's daughter, is directing Frank Asburn—who, we see, is perched high up on a ladder —how to place a legend of evergreens and berries over the chancel arch.

"How is it Mr. Raymond is not here to-night?" Mrs. Wrayton asks.

Mrs. Wrayton is the handsome young wife of Cecil Wrayton, attorney-at-law, and niece of the Rev. John Birch, M.A., vicar of Marton-on-the-Hill.

Mr. and Mrs. Wrayton are Madge Raymond's dearest friends, and Mrs. Wrayton is a little vexed at Madge for not helping them in decorating St. Swithins, as he had promised.

"I really cannot tell," Frank replies, "I've not seen Madge for some days." His real name was Madgwick, a family name.

"I thought you were great friends?" Miss Birch said, interrogatively.

"So we are."

"Then why don't you go and see him; I dare say he's ill?"

"Well, if you particularly wish it, I will—though I don't suppose he's got anything more than an attack of *ennui*."

"You know I don't wish anything of the kind," Minna Birch responded, evidently piqued.

"I don't know anything about it," Frank answers, laughingly; "but now, I think, we've finished. These festoons look very pretty. I wish we could have had a Latin cross done in holly upon the altar—it would have looked so well; only the people here are such red-hot Protestants, I suppose they wouldn't like it."

"Papa would not like anything of that kind on the Communion Table," Minna says, simply.

"Well, we will not argue the point, Miss Birch. I will just step over to Raymond's rooms, and see if anything is the matter. I expect the real fact is that he's forgotten all about decorating the church."

They talk in low tones, as remembering the place they are in.

The party took a last glance at the wreathed columns, the texts done in holly berries, the graceful festoons of laurel, holly, and fir, which coupled the noble Norman pillars together, and the double triangles and other mystic symbols fixed upon the walls, and then left the church.

Miss Birch looked up to see whether Mr. Ashburn would offer to escort her home, or whether she should have to beg the company of Mr. and Mrs. Wrayton back to the vicarage. Frank, however, walked off unceremoniously, evidently in deep thought after bidding them "Good night," and soon solved the question.

Pretty Miss Birch walks silently home with the Wraytons, who wonder why the usually talkative young lady is struck dumb to-night.

Once out in the open street, Mr. Frank strides off to his friend Madge Raymond's lodgings, some quarter of a mile off, and a little way out of the town.

"I wonder whether there's anything up with the fair Marie?"

he asks himself. "What a fool Madge is to allow himself to fall in love with ' sic kittle cattle.' "

The young lady thus alluded to is the *walking lady* at the New Theatre (a very handsome building just erected), a pretty goldenhaired demoiselle, with a very fascinating manner and no heart—who has fairly bewitched Madge, and caused that young gentleman to perform that acrobatic feat known as "falling head over ears in love" with the charming little actress.

If the truth must be told, Madge is not the only one who has been caught in the toils. Half-a-dozen at least of the young men of the best families of Marton have laid their hearts, or at least their purses, at the disposal of the fair Marie Vavasour (real name, Polly Smith). Madge Raymond, however, had been the favoured suitor; and many an envious look had been cast at him, as he entered the boxes at half play of an evening, and Marie, the little flirt, had given him a glance of recognition—half nod, half smile—the moment that she came on the stage in the second piece.

And here let it be said that, coquette as she was, and fond of flattery and presents—especially the latter—no one had ever been known to say a word against her character; for she was very careful in her conduct, and never came to or went from the theatre without her mother or one of the elder ladies of the company as chaperone. Men said of her contemptuously, "Oh, she goes in for matrimony."

Madge Raymond was the nephew of Mr. Brigham, the wealthy town-clerk of Marton, and was understood to be his heir.

It was said of Marton once, by a wag, that it was governed by a Town Council, the Town Council was governed by the Mayor, and the Mayor was governed by the Town Clerk—*ergo*, the Town Clerk was Marton. There was a good deal of truth in this assertion. The town councillors were mostly men of no position, and Mr. Brigham was a clever lawyer, and not without a spice of the *fortiter in re.* He was a bachelor and misogynist, and discouraged the idea of matrimony on the part of his nephew as much as possible.

If the truth must be told, Madge, though now twenty-one, and old enough to know better, was madly in love with the fair actress at the new theatre; and she, finding his intentions were honourable, and being somewhat dubious of the attentions of her other admirers, had encouraged him a good deal, until he, poor fellow, was willing to die for her, like a romantic young fool that he was. Miss Vavasour used to walk out into the country on Sunday afternoons—always, however, accompanied by her mother; and Madge was permitted to join them, which he did with great satisfaction to himself, and greatly to the disgust of the other aspirants to her favour.

Frank Ashburn had often pondered over these things within the last few weeks; and, annoyed though he was at his friend's infatuation, he was determined, if possible, to prevent Madge committing the folly he was evidently contemplating.

Mr. Brigham, too, had been vexed beyond measure at what he heard about his nephew—of course greatly exaggerated by the Marton people, who were celebrated scandal-mongers, and gloated over 'the improper conduct of that wild young man, Mr. Raymond.'

Knowing the great influence Frank had over his nephew, Mr. Brigham called one night unexpectedly at his rooms, and the result of a long conversation was that Frank, by Mr. Brigham's desire, wrote Miss Vavasour a letter—short, sharp, and decisive —which he had duly posted three days ago, and now awaited an answer. Of this, however, Madge knew nothing.

"Mr. Raymond at home?" Frank asks, as he taps at the door of the lodgings in Queen Street, where his friend hangs out.

"No, sir; he hasn't been home since the morning," the girl replies, as she opens the door.

"Pretty looking sort of piece of goods, if she were only washed," Frank thinks, as he surveys the servant, who is housemaid, cook, and boots, and scullery maid all in one,—and pauses for a minute wondering where his friend can be.

"Not in since the morning, and now eleven o'clock. Have you any idea where he is?"

"No, sir."

"I'll go and see if he's at the club;" and off he walks.

"Can't have been such a fool as to run off with that girl," he mutters to himself, as he strides along at a good pace to Charlton Street, where the club is held. "I shouldn't wonder at any folly he might commit, though, by Jove. He certainly is desperately in love with her."

No one has seen him at the club, but some one saw him this evening at the theatre.

Miss Vavasour was not there, however, and her part had been read by the prompter, after the manager had apologised to the audience for her absence—no reason for which, though, had been given.

The next morning, Frank called again at his friend's rooms, but they had heard nothing of him. He could not help feeling somewhat alarmed, and the sight of his expressive countenance quite overcame the Marchioness (they had nicknamed her so after Dickens's Marchioness), who burst into tears, declaring that Mr. Raymond had always been very kind to her, and "she was sure he must be dead, or murdered, or something, because he was always home at nights before."

Having pacified the weeping Abigail, by assuring her that he was sure it was all right, and Mr. Raymond had probably only gone out to spend a day or two with some friends in the country, Frank walked off to church, wondering inwardly whether anything really was the matter, as Madge had promised to dine with him at the Wrayton's that day, and Mr. Brigham was to be there too.

"Here's a pretty kettle of fish," he exclaimed; "and I'll be bound to say it's all my doing. The letter to that girl is at the bottom of it. I'll be hanged if it isn't."

I am afraid Mr. Frank did not enter into the beauty of the glorious service of Christmas Day with that heartiness which was his wont.

After it was over, he called again at Queen Street, and left the Wraytons just after dinner in the evening, to see if his friend had returned; but still no sign.

The next day, too, came and went; and yet no tidings. Sorely perplexed, annoyed, and now really alarmed, he called at the station master's house—for the trains running only as on Sunday, the station was closed; but neither from him nor from any of the police could he glean any tidings of his friend.

Christmas Day did not pass very pleasantly, after all, with some people in Marton.

CHAPTER II.

A MIDNIGHT RIDE.

NEAR to midnight of this Christmas Eve, Mr. Madge Raymond is walking moodily down a lane in the outskirts of Marton, pondering deeply upon something which evidently engages his whole attention, as he stumbles against the solitary wayfarer trudging homeward, who has just crossed the path, and scarcely troubles himself to mutter an apology. As he passes under the last lamp, on the Chilton road, we catch a hasty glimpse of him. Nice-looking enough, certainly; a profusion of light brown hair; by no means despisable whiskers and moustache; a well-knit, if not very robust figure; and a certain gentlemanly bearing, unmistakable in its character, which stamps at once our hero as a well bred young fellow. Handsome, ardent, generous to a fault, hot-blooded, chivalrous, conceited, clever, proud, impulsive; a good friend, a noble enemy; with nothing mean and selfish about him; but open as the day; brave as a lion and gentle as a lamb; frank enough in all that concerned himself, but secret as the night in all that concerned others' confidence entrusted to his keeping; full of little faults and foibles, but with not a particle of vice about the man, — what wonder if he was at once the darling, the hero of the ladies of Marton, the envied rival of the men.

He was so guileless himself, that he believed every woman an angel, and all men honest. Most people liked him, though many looked upon him as a " ne'er do well." He had been a midshipman in the navy, but his father dying at the age of thirty-eight, of consumption (he had married very early in life, and his wife had died in giving birth to Madge), and in very poor circumstances, he left the sea at eighteen, and came to Marton on his uncle's invitation, and was supposed to help him in the office, until he would make up his mind what profession to adopt.

He was an indolent fellow, but did not lack ability; and the great fault of his character seemed to be a want of application and deficiency of ballast. Such was Madge Raymond at the outset of our story.

Madge has received a curious, unsatisfactory note, from Miss Vavasour this morning, bidding him good bye, and telling him that he must never hope to see her again.

The fact of the matter is, that the fair artiste, discovering from Mr. Ashburn's letter—(written, as he informs her, under instructions from Mr. Raymond's uncle and guardian)—that the old gentleman refuses to assist his nephew in any way in the event of his marrying the young actress—such a contemplated step having been hinted to him by Mr. Raymond himself—makes up her mind to accept the son of a wealthy ironmaster, who has proposed to her, and who, fearing that the fickle fair one may change her mind, has persuaded her into an elopement.

Madge had haunted the stage door of the theatre during the morning when rehearsal was on, but saw nothing of the object of his devotion. Directly the doors were opened at night, he had posted himself in the stage box, in hopes of catching a glimpse of Marie before she came on the stage. But again he was disappointed, for no Marie appeared.

Making his way behind as soon as the curtain dropped, he encountered the proprietor—an old gentleman, who had frequently imbibed a friendly glass of something hot at Madge's expense—and from him learnt the tidings, which touched him to the quick, that Miss Vavasour had gone off (as it was said) by the nine o'clock train to Newcastle-under-Lyme, in company with Mr. Shotter, the ironmaster's son.

And this was the end of it all! For the last two months and more he had been following this girl with all the foolish, loving tenderness of a simple, noble faith! Believing nothing of her but what was fair and of good report, shielding her from the wicked flatteries of the designing, and standing forth as her champion in many a fight. The wealth of worship—pure and noble worship—he had bestowed, the love he had cherished, the devotion he had shown, the perseverance with which he had urged his suit, even the costly presents with which he had enriched her and beggared himself, in that short time—these should have pleaded for him, and kept her constant. But no.

She was an actress—a very perfect actress for one so young. She could look and sigh, and murmur "dearest" with the most exquisitely-tender, musical voice, and make poor Madge as happy in the sunshine of her smiles as if all Nature had inspired him to be so; and then, when he was gone, some other favourite was brought forward to be smitten by the same baleful sunstroke.

During the last week or two, Mrs. Vavasour had invited Madge to come and take tea with them three or four times; and, now that an understanding had grown up between the two, and it was understood Madge would marry her if his uncle would only do something for him, he had been allowed to wait for Marie and escort her home after the play was over.

Madge had not yet actually asked his uncle's consent, if the truth must be told, being afraid; but he had made no secret of his intention, and so the matter had got to the old man's ears. William Brigham, rightly enough, conjectured that if he was too severe with his nephew, he might do something foolish and run away with the girl, who no doubt would marry him if she saw any prospect of his (Mr. Brigham's) assisting them. So he thought it best to confer with Madge's old friend, young Ashburn, who was his senior by some six or seven years, and a sensible, quiet, and gentlemanly man of the world. The result was, as we have seen, Miss Vavasour had eloped, and her lover left to wear the willow. Christmas Eve is not a happy one to him.

It is now midnight. The bells of St. Swithin have just chimed out the quarters, and now the great bell is striking the hour. It has been a lovely moonlight night; but the wind has risen, and the sky is now covered with clouds. There will be a snow-storm presently. Not a soul to be seen — nothing stirring save the wind.

Far down the lane the railroad crosses the highway; the gates are open though, now; and but for the red lamps placed on the posts, which somewhat dimly lights the way, you would not know you were near a railway, so dark and silent is all around. Utterly careless as to what becomes of him, frenzied with rage at Marie's perfidy, and perhaps suffering from the effects of the drink he had been foolishly imbibing to drive dull care away, Madge strides hastily along the road, perfectly indifferent as to where he is going. The crossing is not a hundred yards from the station; and as he approaches, the gates swing back, and a long train of empty carriages, which have brought excursionists down to the cattle show, just over, moves out of the station, and approaches the spot where Madge is standing, close to the gates. A sudden whim comes over him to see where the train is going, probably to shunt at the points some half a mile down the line, as he thinks. No sooner said than done. As the train slowly passes, it is a comparatively easy matter to jump up upon the foot-boards of one of the carriages, and hold on to the rail which girds the carriage—a third-class one. Our hero is somewhat dismayed, however, to find that the train does not slacken speed at the junction at Low Marton, but, with a sharp whistle from the engine, rattles through the station, and dashes forward on its way, increasing in pace every moment. With wonderful coolness and pluck—all his faculties restored by the sense of danger—he cautiously walks along the foot-rail of three or four of the carriages, stretching forward, clutching the handles of the doors, which are five feet apart, to sustain him, as there is no hand-rail to any but the third-class carriages, and so makes his way forward to the front of the train. His object is to get as far as the engine, if possible, though there are something like thirty carriages in all, and he is not a sixth part of the way up yet.

A whirr—a crash—a blinding light—a scream, and they have passed Shrival station, and on again—going at a speed of thirty miles an hour. It is useless now to hope to stop the train, as he would now be too far from home to be able to walk there to-night. Then he tries to get in at one of the carriages. But the doors are all locked. Just now they are swinging round the curve at Weltham, and speed is slackened. Madge just grazes a telegraph post as they pass, and begins to feel that his position is by no means a pleasant one. It is now very cold, and he feels that he cannot hold on to the door handle much longer, his hands have become so numb. To leap down at the speed at which they are going would be madness; besides, it's so dark you couldn't see two yards before you. If he could only get to the top of one of the carriages, he would be safer there.

Rattle-rattle — thud-thud — clatter-clatter — the great engine pounds its way along the iron highway, wallowing in fire and water, and vomiting forth its flame and smoke; screaming past station after station, like some horrid fiend, making night hideous with its unearthly music.

A train rushing through a station at full speed at the dead of night is not a pleasant subject to contemplate, at least to our thinking. Mogford is now passed; we are fifteen miles from Marton, and still no appearance of stopping. Another ten minutes of gloom, and we have gone over nearly as many miles. Ruswarp is in view, and we have got out of the high bleak flat country into the midst of the hills near Congleton Edge. A light break in the clouds helps Madge to see his way, and he cautiously, but surely, makes his way round to the side of the carriage on which he is standing, and proceeds to mount on to the buffers, and from thence to the seat on the top.

Oh, horrors; he has slipped!

A cloud passes over the moon, and the train is enshrouded in darkness. Another drifting of the heavy mass of vapour now falling in snow flakes, and we see, by the dim light, Madge hanging by his hands to the little rail which surrounds the seat on the top of the carriage, and struggling to obtain a foothold. A moment, and it is done, and now he has managed to clamber up, and is seated upon the carriage top, as coolly as if it was an every day matter with him.

"By Jove, I was nearly done for, that time. I wonder if I shall ever get home again. Here's a pretty go," our hero ejaculated, as he makes himself as comfortable as he can in such a particularly airy situation.

"Hollo, here's a tunnel. I suppose I must duck," and down he bends, holding on by his hands at the sides, and bending himself double as the train dashes under an arch.

"Not a tunnel after all, only a viaduct. I needn't have ducked for that, unless to learn the *via*. That's a pun, by the way: fancy a fellow punning in such a position as I am." And the young fellow burst out into a hearty laugh at the incongruity of the thing.

Cold, dreadfully cold; dark, pitchy dark. Only now and then, as a station is passed, the flash of a passing signal-lamp lights up the train as it whirls by, and shows it crusted with a covering of snow, driving along at forty miles per hour.

And now Madge knows they must be approaching the great tunnel which is cut through Boughton Edge, and begins to think seriously of what he should do. The Elton Bridge tunnel is one of the lowest in England, and it is very doubtful if any ordinary-sized man, sitting upright upon the top of a carriage, could pass under in safety.

Whirr-whirr—clatter-clatter—thud-thud—the train dashes onward through the dead of night, over a snow-clad earth under a gloomy sky.

A sudden break in the cloud reveals to him the approaching danger from the tunnel. Again he bends forward and lies low; and with a screech and a roar, the train dashes into the stifling cavernous darkness—the lamps casting a lurid glare on its rugged walls, "not light, but only darkness visible"—and through it and into the night air again.

His cane, which he had carelessly stuck into one of the lamps, is snapped in half—the two pieces, however, lie on the top of the carriage.

"Confound it," the young gentleman says, as he observes this, "got smashed because I stuck it upright in that pepper castor. Let's see what the height of the thing would be beside me. By Jove, only half an inch difference between us. So! I suppose if I had not seen the tunnel, and bobbed down in time, my head would have been smashed. Hang it all, I am getting tired of this lark. I wonder how long it's going to last, and where the dickens I am going to. I'll try what a cigar will do. What a fool I was not to think of that before. It's confoundedly cold."

On again, but sensible diminution of speed.

"We are getting to Macclesfield, fifty miles from home. Well, that's a caution. Wonder if it will stop here? Hope so. Hang that girl!"

The train does stop, luckily for our hero, and he dismounts

from his dangerous pedestal, thanking his stars that he's got safe to *terra firma* again.

Light hearted fellow though he is, he is somewhat sobered by this night's journey; and the midnight ride has affected him more than he cares to own.

Making his way as best he can, half-starved with the cold as he is, and by no means desirous of being seen by the guard or porter in charge of the train, he finds his way to an inn, knocks up the inmates, at last gains admission, and is soon in the arms of Morpheus.

The next morning—Christmas morning—he is in a high state of fever, brought on by exposure to the cold. The following day he is worse, and sends off for his friend Ashburn. The third day he is delirious, and raving about Marie.

CHAPTER III.

EXPLANATORY.—TEMPORA MUTANTUR.

Mr. Ashburn is one of the firm of Wrayton and Ashburn, solicitors.

It is Thursday morning, two days after Christmas Day; and Frank is sitting chatting pleasantly to dear Mrs. Wrayton, who is pouring out her husband's coffee—he, lazy fellow, not down yet.

"No letters come yet, Mrs. Wrayton? I thought I'd step down to see if there were any on my way to the office. I am getting anxious about Raymond"—(Frank has had no letters addressed here lately).

A servant enters while he is speaking, and hands the letters to her mistress, who reads aloud the addresses—"Mrs. Cecil Wrayton," "Mrs. C. Wrayton," "Messrs. Wrayton and Ashburn," "Frank Ashburn, Esq., care of Messrs. Wrayton and Ashburn."

"What a queer way of addressing you, and what a queer hand! Here, there are a great many more. Cecil wont be angry with me for looking over his letters first; but I expected a reply from Miss Edwardes, my husband's cousin, whom we had asked to come and stay with us this Christmas. She ought to have been here a week ago. Such a pretty girl, Mr. Ashburn; and money, too, I believe. I must introduce you two. I dare say you would suit each other."

"Thanks; but I am afraid I might not prove so impressible as you think, nor the lady either; and, besides, I don't believe in marrying for money."

"Don't you? I thought you did, as you have never married yet."

"Is not that woman's logic? I am too poor to think of such a luxury as matrimony; and the mere fact of the lady whom I love being rich would be, I am afraid, a great barrier to my proposing, since I should be sure she would think I wanted to marry her only for her money."

"That would all depend upon the girl herself. If I had been ever so rich, I should not have thought Cecil married me for my money."

"Oh, that's a different thing, you are so——," and here Frank paused.

He did not want to offend Mrs. Wrayton by flattering her; and yet he was just on the point of saying something which was very complimentary indeed, but stopped himself, and added, "I mean you are so nice, and kind, and attractive, and all that sort of thing."

"Thank you, you are good enough to say so. Oh, I forgot to give you the letter. I hope there is news from Mr. Raymond;" and Mrs. Wrayton, failing to find a reply from Miss Edwardes, gave the bundle to Frank, who soon singled out two from the heap. Hastily opening the first he read as follows:—

"Nags Head, Macclesfield, 26th Dec., 1859.

"My Dear Ashburn,—

"I am rather poorly. Please come to see me. I hope I am not going to be laid up.—Yours, in haste,

"Madge Raymond.

"P.S.—Tell the Wraytons, but don't alarm my uncle."

The other letter, the one Mrs. Wrayton had noticed as peculiarly written, was from Miss Vavasour. It was not pleasantly written, and is not worth reproducing here; and Frank crumpled it up in his pocket, apologised to Mrs. Wrayton for going directly, desired her to explain to her husband, and left the house.

"I wonder whether he cares for Minna?" Mrs. Wrayton says, thoughtfully.

"What can be the matter with Mr. Raymond?—I'll go at once. I hope the boy isn't ill. How on earth has he got Macclesfield? I wish he were more careful of himself; he'll go off in a consumption one of these days." Thus spoke Frank as he paced thoughtfully down the street.

By mid-day he was at Macclesfield, and found poor Madge very ill. He had not even gone home to take anything, but had just walked off to the station from the office with a small valise, which he generally kept there, containing such necessaries as a bachelor usually carries about with him.

And Madge raved about Marie!

As his friend heard him, he wished most devoutly he had had nothing to do with the letter, which at Mr. Brigham's dictation he had written to her.

In three weeks time, however, Madge was well enough to be removed; and Frank, who had stayed with him a week of that time, but had now gone down to Marton, returned to take him back.

"Put on my great coat; yours is not warm enough, and you mustn't catch cold," Frank said, as he assisted his friend to attire himself this fine frosty morning, in the middle of January, 1860, and helped him into the cab which was to take them to the station.

Master Madge Raymond is not the better for his midnight ride.

One evening they are sitting talking together over the fire, in Madge's rooms, and Madge is railing against women in general, and actresses in particular.

"They are all the same—false and fickle, fickle and false."

"There you are wrong," Frank says, quietly. "I have known actresses as pure and noble characters as you would find anywhere; women who would adorn any society, no matter how high, no matter how virtuous. You have no right to judge of a class by a single specimen."

"And pray, where did you gain your experience of them, most sapient judge?"

"Never mind; I am not going to confess to you, my boy. But you must remember I've not been in Marton all my life. Well, I must be off; I have an engagement at eight. Ah! I see my great coat is here; I was wondering where it was. It's a fine night, I think I'll leave it here. Good night, old fellow. Don't become a misogynist." So saying, off he went, leaving Madge ruminating over the fire.

"How the old fellow fired up when I spoke about actresses! What the dickens was it made that girl leave me in the lurch as she did? What a fool I was to think so much about her! I wish to goodness I could forget her. I think I'll have a smoke." He got up and felt in the pocket of Frank's great coat, where he had put half-a-dozen cigars; and, in taking one from its depth, brought out a crumpled-up note, which he was just going to consign to the flames as rubbish, when his own name in it caught his eye. The signature, "Marie Vavasour," caused him to open and read it without hesitation; and, I am afraid, he muttered something very like an oath as he finished it.

"Cool of that fellow, Ashburn, to interfere in my business. So, that's the reading of the riddle, is it? I'll not stand it; I'm hanged if I do."

The young gentleman had worked himself up into a rage, and perhaps it was as well that Frank Ashburn did not come in just then.

They quarrelled, and Frank tried to explain—but Madge would hear nothing.

"It was a confounded shame," he said, "for a man who called himself his friend to interfere in his business in such an unwarrantable and impertinent manner as Ashburn had done."

They parted—Frank, " more in sorrow than in anger."

Two years have rolled away, Madge has not improved. He has got the character of being a great flirt; and, wanting the advice and council of his friend to steer him, he has grown rather wild. Not that he does anything very wrong, but that he does nothing good. He has got the character of being fickle, too, and his uncle is in hopes he will become, as he is striving to become, a *woman hater*. It was a long time before he recovered from the effects of his wild night's excursion. It was feared that his lungs were affected, and he has not yet got so strong as could be wished.

It is now the summer of 1863. Madge has long since forgotten Marie, and would like to make it up again with Frank, but he is too proud to ask forgiveness. Frank, on the other hand, is equally desirous that their old friendship should be renewed; but he disapproves of so many things Madge has done lately, and feels that he is of such an uncertain and changeable disposition, that, if he offered him advice, there might only arise other differences, and then they might quarrel again.

A new company has just been formed, and Mr. Brigham, who has invested a good deal of money in it, is made a director. He has always looked upon himself as under obligations to Frank for the part he took about the fair Marie. Since then, they have had frequent intercourse together in business matters. Mr. Brigham has put many things into his young friend's way, as magistrates' clerk, and thinks very highly of his talents. The directors are looking out for a secretary, and Mr. Brigham proposes Mr. Ashburn; but to the astonishment of the worthy town clerk he declines.

"Why, my dear fellow," Mr. Brigham says, "it's £500 a-year, and very likely will increase as the company prospers. You don't make such an income now?"

"No; I am only junior partner, and I have far less than that, certainly; still, I am fond of my profession, and should not like to leave it, and I think I would rather not take it, though I am very much obliged to you, Mr. Brigham, for all your kindness."

"I am glad you like your profession. No man ever got on who did not like his calling."

"If you will allow me, I will recommend a friend of my own, who, I think, would suit you," Frank pleaded.

"And who may that be, sir?" the old man says, somewhat testily.

"Your nephew, sir."

"My nephew, sir! He is far too wild."

"That is only for want of occupation. Put him in a position of responsibility, and make him feel that everything depends upon his conduct; and, rely upon it, he has some good stuff in him, and he will do you no discredit."

"You are very good to speak so well of Madge, Mr. Ashburn; but I thought you and he were not very good friends?"

"Well, sir, the quarrelling is on his side, not mine."

"He is not very strong at present, I believe," Mr. Brigham says, after a pause. "I am afraid I've rather neglected him. Poor fellow, he's never known a father's care or a mother's love. My sister was the only woman I ever knew worth caring for. I'll send him off to Killarney for a month or two, to see what that will do for him—and then, if he's pretty strong again, and takes to the idea, I'll see about the secretaryship. We shan't be in full working order for three months yet, so there's plenty of time. I'll take care to let my nephew know at whose recommendation he gets the post," Mr. Brigham added. "Good morning, Mr. Ashburn."

"Good morning," and they part.

Frank feels very much better after this, and does not now regret the share he had in Madge's discomfiture, since he sees good may come out of it after all.

CHAPTER IV.

RECONCILIATION.

"Dear old boy, I am so glad we have made it all up. I've often wished to ask you to be friends again, but I was too proud."

It is Madge Raymond who is speaking, and they are in Frank's room, having a cosy dinner—a fortnight after the events in the last chapter.

Mr. Brigham had sent for Madge specially, to tell him that his friend Frank Ashburn had declined, in his favour, a situation he meant to give him; and took the opportunity of expatiating upon the sentiments of friendship which Mr. Ashburn had expressed, until poor Madge began to feel heartily ashamed of himself for ever bearing malice against a friend who had evidently ever borne *his* real interest at heart; and so, briefly thanking his uncle for his kindness, he, impulsive, generous, high-souled fellow as he was, went straight to Frank Asburn's room, and begged for forgiveness of all his folly and petulance. The tears stood in Frank's eyes as he warmly shook his hand; and those two were happier in their reconciliation that evening than either of them had been for this many a day. Of course, they ratified the renewal of friendship with an interchange of dinners—they would hardly have been English not to do so; and now they are chatting away in Frank's room, over a bottle of wine and some strawberries; and Madge is building castles in the air.

"My uncle did not say exactly what this place was he was going to give me. Perhaps he's not certain of getting it, and so does not want to disappoint me. I shall be glad to get some settled work, you know, Frank. My uncle, he's a very good fellow, you know; I don't want to say a word against him; but he's let me have my own way so much, that I'm scarcely fit for anything, you know. I've gone in and out of the office just as I have liked, done as little or as much work as I chose—uncle Brigham has taken no notice of me. If I worked hard he never praised me; if I did nothing he never complained. I just received my £150 a year, and that was all about it."

"Well, my boy, you must settle down now," Frank says, gravely.

"Oh, yes, I mean to. But I don't think my uncle would have cared much if I had gone to the devil."

"You are wrong there, I think. Your uncle is peculiar, perhaps, in his views, especially as regards the ladies; but I am sure he wishes you well."

"Give us a cigar. Thanks. Very good one, this. Where did you get it?" and Frank puffs away for a minute or two, and then says,

"I say, Madge, why don't you get married?"

"Married, my dear fellow? Why, I'm only twenty-four—I might say *tu quoque* to that."

"Oh, with me it's a different matter; I'm too poor at present;—you have your uncle to back you."

"Not in the matrimonial line, though. I mean to marry for money when I do commit the deed. I'll trouble you for the wine—it's with you. Thanks, half a glass will do; I can't stand much."

"You mean to marry for money, do you?" Frank answers, meditatively knocking the ash off the end of his cigar, against the fireplace as he speaks.

"Yes, I think so. Why not?"

"Take my advice, Madge—don't."

"Well, what's a fellow to do?"

"Work, my boy, work! If you can't maintain a wife by your own exertions—aye, and as a lady, too—you are not the man I took you for."

"Oh, it's all very well to say so. If a fellow were awfully in love with a girl, I dare say he might do something; but I shall never love again. Besides, supposing I should fall in love with a girl who had tin, how then?" Madge continued.

"Well, with your avowed sentiments and your character as a flirt—don't wince—it would be awkward, as, no doubt, the lady would think you approached her for her money. In that case, I suppose you could only trust to time, and to your own devotion, to prove you loved her for herself alone. Besides if a girl is clever and good looking, she has no right to think you make love to her for the *filthy lucre*. If she is ugly, it's a different matter. By the way, Madge, you are going to Killarney, are you not?"

"Yes, to-morrow."

"Very likely you'll meet with some fair 'Norah Creina' there who'll steal your heart away."

"Oh, I'm not likely to fall in love with an Irish girl."

"Well, I don't know. I think very likely you will fall in love, and *hopelessly*."

CHAPTER V.

MAY EDWARDES.—THE CONCLUSION.

Letter from Madge Raymond, Esq., to his friend Frank Ashburn, Esq.

"Lake Hotel, Killarney, 24th July, 1863.
"My Dear old Boy,—
"You are a prophet, and no mistake. I dare say you have been wondering why I have been here three weeks, and yet have never written to you. You'll never guess the cause, so I will tell you. I've actually fallen in love. Such a glorious girl —you can't think. We were saying, only the other day, how hard it was for a fellow to be a hero now-a-days. Nobody had a chance, except in a novel, of showing how he loved a girl, or anything of that sort. But fortune favoured me; and I'll tell you, as briefly as I can, all about it.

"Yesterday week a party put up here—a Sir William Edwardes and his wife; two daughters, rather plain; and two nieces, one very pretty. He is an old baronet of Charles I.'s creation (the title must be about contemporary with your cousin's), but I fancy he's rather poor. One of the nieces—the one I am going to tell you about—is an heiress; so I am told. Her name is Marian Wentworth Edwardes, but they always call her May. Such a pretty girl! Exquisite complexion—pink and white; black hair, worn rather short, and one mass of ringlets; fine arched pencilled brows; glorious, flashing, large brown eyes, the most expressive I ever saw; a pretty mouth, evidently meant for kisses; and pearly teeth. She is rather under the middle height, has pretty hands and feet, the sweetest and most musical voice I ever heard, and the most charming accent (not brogue, mark me) I ever heard from the lips of a lady.

"The Irish ladies are very nice, and May Edwardes is the most fascinating little piece of goods I ever met. So much for her. The old fellow was very jolly and agreeable, and we got on very well together. They live somewhere in Galway, I believe; and, strange to say, had never seen Killarney before; so I volunteered to be their *cicerone*. We went, of course, through the Gap of Dunloe, and down the lakes. Then, the second day, I took them up Mangerton. Another day, we went through Colonel Herbert of Muckross's estate, and so forth, and through the lakes that way.

"The Irish are not awfully stiff, consequential, and reserved, as we English are: and in a few days I was as intimate as possible with them. I happened to mention Marton, and Miss Edwardes (*my* Miss Edwardes) said she knew the Wraytons there; and, if I remember right, added that your partner was her cousin. She said she had had a letter from Mrs. Wrayton, only a week or two since, asking her to come and stay with them; that it was the second invitation she had had, but was afraid she should have to decline it.

"Well, last Friday evening, some one proposed we should visit Innisfallen by moonlight. Lady Edwardes would not go, but Sir William accompanied us. We got to Innisfallen, admired the ruined chapel, explored the island, and, on returning, Miss Edwardes missed her brooch, which she fancied she must have dropped at the other end of the island, near the part called the Bed of Honour—the Duke of Rutland's resting-place when he was Lord-Lieutenant. The rest of the party wanted to go over to see Ross Castle—from which Lord Castle Rosse takes his title

—a fine old ruin on the mainland, a very little distance from Innisfallen, and so left Miss Edwardes, myself, and Sir William's two sons—lads of about fourteen and twelve—to look for the brooch until their return. We had just got to a point from which there is a lovely view of the lakes, with the Purple Mountain in front of us, and Mangerton standing sentinel gloomily behind, when I heard a scream, and looking round, found that May had slipped, and had fallen into the water. Hastily pulling my coat off, I jumped in, and before she sank for the third time, caught hold of her, and, thank God, brought her to land before life was quite extinct. William Edwardes ran off at once for assistance, leaving me, as best I could, to apply what restoratives I could think of. Luckily I had a small flask of brandy with me, and after giving her a little, she revived. It was half an hour before they came.

"Such delicious terror I never experienced before. As I held the poor child in my arms, and tried to bring her back to life, I felt that perhaps, after all, it might be happier for me to die thus. We got her home at last. She has been confined to her room ever since, but got up to-day for the first time. I have had a slight cold, but am otherwise no worse.

"I shall never forget her sweet pale face—oh, so dead pale—turned up to heaven, with the moonbeams smiling sadly upon it, as I placed her on the bank, and covered her with my coat and a shawl we had, and watched and waited till help should come. She looked so like an angel asleep.

"I can't write any more just now.—Yours ever,

"MADGE."

Letter from Miss May Edwardes to Mrs. Cecil Wrayton.
"MY DEAR MRS. WRAYTON,—

"A thousand thanks for your kind invitation. I will

really come to Marton very soon, but just at present I can't come, for I have hardly recovered yet from an accident which happened to me on Friday. I will write again in a few days, but I know you will forgive me writing more at present, as I am not by any means well yet, and very little tires me.

"Give my kindest love to Cousin Cecil, and believe me, my dear Mrs. Wrayton, very affectionately yours,

"MAY EDWARDES.

"P.S.—A Mr. Raymond is staying here now, who talks of you and Cecil very warmly. My uncle and cousins like him very much; and I owe my life to him."

It was not till Frank and Mrs. Wrayton compared notes that they came to a right conclusion as to the meaning of the two epistles above quoted.

In another fortnight Madge returned. He and his friend were discussing matters matrimonial a few evenings afterwards, when Madge said,

"Confound it all. I wish she were not rich."

"And who, pray, is *she?*" Frank asks, provokingly.

"Oh, you know who I mean."

"Well, if you mean Miss Edwardes, may I be permitted to ask how do you know that she is rich?"

"Well, somebody said that Sir William Edwardes' niece was an heiress."

"So she is; but it is the other one, Miss Barham."

"Are you sure?"

"Certain."

"Well, then, I'm glad to hear it. Give us your hand, old fellow, you've made me so happy."

"How now? I thought you were going to marry for money."

"Oh, hang money!"

"Well, have you spoken to Sir William? You know he's her guardian."

"No, I haven't;"—and a cloud came over the expressive face of her hero. "I suppose he won't have me because I'm no great catch, and our family never were anybody. I say, Frank, yours is a good family, isn't it?"

"Pretty fair, I believe. We were barons in Edward III.'s time."

"Wish I were of good family. We are nobody, you know. I doubt if I had a grandfather."

"My dear boy, unless you are a duke, or a lord at least, good family goes for nothing now-a-days. People take you for what you *are*, not for what you *were*. No one cares a jot who your ancestors were. The question is, 'What are you worth?' Go in and win, my boy, go in and win. Your uncle has given you this secretaryship."

"Dear old Frank,—you are a good fellow. If I do succeed, I'm sure I shall have you to thank for it."

*   *   *   *   *   *

Christmas has come round again—the Christmas of 1865. Pretty May Edwardes is now Mrs. Madge Raymond. They are sitting over their Christmas dinner—or rather dessert—and Uncle Brigham is there. He has been heard to declare that, if there was ever any woman in the world worth caring for, besides his sister, it is Mrs. Madge Raymond.

"And so, May, that was *my* midnight's ride," Madge is saying, as he concludes the account of the adventure related in these pages.

"Well, it's all very wonderful, dear; and I'm glad, after all, you had that adventure."

"Why?"

"Because, if you had not, you would not have been ill, and

you would not have gone to Killarney for your health; and then you would not have seen poor little me, would you?"

Uncle Brigham is having a quiet nap over the fire, with his handkerchief over his face.

"Did you really fall in love with me at first sight?" May says again, presently, for the thousandth time, at least, since they have been married.

Madge came round and answered her by putting his arms round her waist, and lifting up her face to his, as he gazed into those truthful eyes of hers with a look of infinite tenderness, and answered, as he kissed her,

"Yes, darling, who could help loving you? I loved you from the first—passionately—*Hopelessly!*"

"God knows how I thank Him every hour for such a blessing as you are," May says, after a long pause, her eyes moistening as she spoke.

"You will be glad to hear, dear, that Mr. Birch has at length given his consent to the match between Minna and your friend Mr. Ashburn. I am very glad. I think he was *hopelessly* in love with her, dear old fellow."

"Yes, dear; but it will not now, you know, be *Hopelessly!*"

THE END.

OLD TRUTHS.

There are women will not pry;
There are babes who never cry;
There are men who will not lie;
There be names that will not die.

There are deeds that leave no stain,
Yet are fruitful source of pain;
There are things we cannot see,
Yet exist or are to be.

There is that without a name
Brings upon it nought but shame;
In this old mortality,
Nought so great as chastity.

MASONIC PAPERS.

NOTES ON THE OLD MINUTE BOOKS OF THE BRITISH UNION LODGE, No. 114, IPSWICH. A.D., 1762.

FIRST MINUTE BOOK.

A VERY interesting book is the first Minute Book of this old Lodge, though it has seen much service and fared ill in the hands it has passed through. It seems to have got into the possession of some cowan, and to have been given over to the tender mercies of some child or children, for almost every leaf has a piece snipped out of it, and youthful scrawls and attempts at caligraphy disfigure almost every page.

The first page in the book (apparently one is lost), which is dated 5th April, 1762, contains a part of the 3rd rule, or by-law, which has reference to the ballot; white and black beans being used, as at present, in determining the important question as to whether a candidate should or should not be received into the time-honoured fraternity.

"Fourthly," runs the rule, "That after every brother has put in a bean as directed, the box be then delivered to the master, by the secretary, for his inspection. Fifthly and lastly—that if the master find a black bean in the box, no further mention shall be made to the intended member."

A very considerate rule this last, and one which might be more generally adopted than it is. The secrecy of the ballot I have known to be "more honoured in the breach than the observance," though not in the lodge of which I am writing.

And touching this said system of ballot, it would be well if there were some fixed rule as to how it should be exercised. In England an entered apprentice can exercise his right of voting on any question before the lodge, from the election of W.M. to the admission of a candidate to the mysteries and privileges of Freemasonry. In America, I believe, it is different; no brother can vote until he is a Master Mason.

In England the ceremony of voting differed in different lodges. In some the deacon carried round the ballot box to each member, and a most objectionable practice, since the officer could hardly fail to see how the brother voted, and the secrecy of the ballot became a farce. In other lodges the brethren went indiscriminately, and all in a heap, up to the treasurer's desk, and thus confusion was made, and the importance of the ballot was not impressed on the neophyte by a ceremony which should always be done "decently and in order."

But to return to the British Union and its first record of minutes. This volume appears to have served the double purpose of a minute and presence book, and underneath the by-laws quoted we have the signatures of the brethren present.

John Clarke, Master; John Hunter, Senior Warden; W. Clarke, Junior Warden; John Prentice, Stephen Buston, Thos. R. Scott, John Concour, Joseph Clarke, Wm. Prentice. There is no date to this meeting, but the next one is dated 5th April, 1762, when, in addition to the names mentioned above, there appear to have been two visitors present, Jonas Philips and Marchal Calksen, the latter probably a foreigner. A note is put at the bottom of the entry to the effect that a certain brother, whose name has been cut out, being absent, forfeits sixpence. The next meeting appears to have been held 19th April, 1762.

At this lodge Bros. Thos. Nichol-Scott, John Clarke and John Concour were raised Masters; and there is a N.B. that certain of the brethren, all but the visitors and candidates in fact, each paid sixpence, we will suppose for refreshment.

At the meeting dated 17th May, 1762, only four brethren appear to have been present, and the lodge seems to have been under the rule of the J.W., neither the W.M. nor S.W. being there.

At a lodge held on the 21st June, Wm. Paxman was proposed for ballot on St. John's day, together with Robert Fenn, and accordingly on the 24th June it appears they were regularly made, agreeable to the by-laws heretofore entered in this book. At the same time John Hunter was, with the unanimous consent of this lodge, elected Master for the ensuing half-year, Wm. Clarke, S.W., and J. Prentice, J.W. of the lodge. This is a very interesting minute, since it would appear that a century ago the Master was, occasionally at least, elected half-yearly, and the Wardens, instead of being the nominees of the Master, were, like himself, elected by the brethren.

At the next lodge meeting, John Hunter's name appears as Master, and John Clarke's as P.M.; but there is nothing to show that there was any special ceremony in inducting the new W.M. into the chair of K.S., though I should be sorry to assert, as some of the exact writers on Masonic subjects would, that the mere absence of mention of the admitting to the installed Master's degree, was proof positive that no such degree existed at this time.

On the 2nd August, 1762, the Master appears to have been amongst the absentees, and John Clarke signs as D. Master, both on this and the following lodge night. Depute Master is quite a Scotch "style," and I never remember to have seen it in an English minute book before. A Captain John Softly, of Sunder-

land, no doubt in the merchantile service, was regularly made on
this occasion. Robert Fenn appears to have served the office of
Tyler at this time. A Mr. Wm. Enefer, of Harwich, was duly
admitted a brother on the 15th November, 1762, and raised a
fellowcraft the same night. This seems to have been a common
practice to give the two degrees in one night, for on the very
next lodge night Mr. John Bailey, of Harwich, was duly admitted
a brother, and raised fellowcraft. At this time the Master is des-
cribed as Right Worshipful, a term now only applied to Provin-
cial Grand Masters in this country, though in Scotland the
holder of the gavel is still described as R.W.M. Right Worship-
ful, by the way, is, if I mistake not, the style of a Knight, whilst
Worshipful is that of an Esquire. The former is still used, we
believe, by some of the Mayors of our older corporations in the
great cities, by the Vicar General of the Province of Canterbury,
and the Judge of the Bishop of London's Consistory Court,
though the latter is the more usual title assumed by Mayors and
Aldermen, and, I believe, the Masters of the City Livery Com-
panies, the relics of the trade guilds of the middle ages. Accord-
ing to Burke, Mayors of boroughs and Justices of the Peace are
Esquires by virtue of their office; so are servants of the Crown,
holding responsible and independent positions, and it is on this
ground that magistrates are always addressed as " Your Wor-
ship." The modern fashion of dubbing everybody Esquire who
does not actually keep a shop, is as ridiculous as the *servant-
galism* of the day whose representatives have their letters ad-
dressed *Miss*, and speak of each other as " me and another
young lady." But I am sadly digressing from the title Worship-
ful. Does it not suggest itself to my brethren that the mere title
accorded to a Master shows that his position as such was con-
sidered a century ago, and should be now, as one of very high
importance in the craft; and, as in choosing the Mayor of a

town, it is generally the most distinguished citizen who can be prevailed upon to take the office who is selected to fill the post, and the one whose means, social position, or great talent justify the selection; so in Masonry, we should always be careful to put into office brethren to whom the title Worshipful might properly be applied, without raising a sneer from the outside world at its application to a brother who fails to dignify the office, either by his capacity, his character, or his position in society. But this is a digression which, in later years, at all events, could have no possible application so far as the British Union Lodge is concerned; a lodge which at the present time occupies the first position in the province of Suffolk, and compares favourably in the social status of its members with almost any lodge in England. Recurring to my notes of the British Union, I find that Bro. Wm. Clarke was unanimously chosen Master at the St. John's Festival, 27th December, 1762, at which time the Wardens were also elected. The names of brethren absent appear to be regularly recorded, and against their names at the January meeting in 1763 I find that the forfeits are to be paid the first night when present.

Whether a recurrence to this good, old practice would secure a more regular attendance at lodge meetings, I do not know, and, perhaps, so far as the members generally are concerned, it would be unwise to revive the rule; but with regard to office-bearers it is a matter for consideration for the craft generally whether a fine (*which should invariably be enforced*) inflicted upon all officers absent at regular lodge meetings would not be a sure way of securing really good officers, and good working. Of course sickness, the pressing emergencies of public or private avocations, would be always fairly considered; but these apart, brethren who willingly accept office should be made to fulfil the duties appertaining thereto.

At the lodge meeting held on the 5th February, 1763, Mr.

George Ward and Mr. John Watson, of Harwich, were proposed to be admitted brethren, and the latter appears to have been initiated and admitted to the second degree of Masonry the following lodge night.

At this time it was "ordered by the lodge that no person be ever proposed for being made a brother unless the proposing brother will promise to pay the usual admittance fee of a guinea," [the full amount charged for initiation at that time] "in case the person so proposed should fail attending at the time then fixed for his making, unless a satisfactory reason be given for his non-attendance." It would be well if this rule were enforced now generally. No candidate should ever be allowed to be proposed until the proposition fee, *obtained from him*, and *not* advanced by the proposer, be paid. A great deal of unnecessary trouble and annoyance would be spared if this admirable by-law were at all times strictly enforced.

On the 3rd October, 1763, Bros. William Prentice, William Paxman and Robert Fenn were raised Masters. The last two of these brethren had been made August, 1762, and it would be worth knowing whether a year was required to elapse between the passing and raising, as at present practised in some countries, and notably, I believe in Prussia. There is a regular record of visitors' names at this period, but nothing to show from what lodges they hailed.

At the St. John's Festival, 27th December, 1763, Bros. William Enefer, John Watson and Richard Bennett were raised Masters. Watson had been initiated and admitted to the second degree of Masonry, February, 1763; Enefer had been "admitted a brother and raised a fellowcraft," November, 1762, by which we may conclude that a much longer interval elapsed between the passing and raising than is now deemed necessary, in the one case ten months, and in the other more than twelve months being the period allowed to pass before the brethren were deemed eligible for the Master's degree. It does not appear, however, that there was any fixed rule upon the subject. Bro. James Clements, a visitor who had previously attended the lodge in October, 1763, was " raised a Master " at the lodge meeting, 20th February, 1764. At the previous lodge William Swain, schoolmaster, of Woodbridge, was balloted for, and unanimously approved of, for initiation ; and at the following one Gardiner Whiteside, of Yarmouth Ship (probably a publican, let us hope not a sinner), was duly balloted for, and was made the next meeting.

In June, 1764, Thos. Buck was balloted for, accepted, and " immediately raised a fellowcraft," the term *passed* apparently not being used at this period. Several foreigners appear to have visited the British Union from time to time, as we may gather from the mention of such visiting brethren as Peter Mitaux, who subsequently joined the lodge, Benjamin Didior, Jasper Fatay (in another place spelt Faetus), Arnold Grownwald, &c.

Gardiner Whiteside, made in June, was raised to the third degree of Masonry in September, 1764, which seems conclusively to show that there was no settled rule as to the limit of time between conferring the degrees longer than that allowed by the Book of Constitutions.

On the 17th December, 1764, there were four visitors present, hailing respectively from S*t*. John's (we presume New Brunswick), Sunderland, Norwich and Harwich. This is the first notice of the locality from whence the visiting brethren came.

A regular record appears throughout of the absentees as well as of those present.

At the meeting held December, 1765, we find the record of the names of the Master, Wardens and Tyler, who were all elected by the lodge.

At the meeting held 7th December, 1767, William Kolly, a

vizitant (sic) brother, and Thomas Woodwards, Peter Wooton, William Clarke, Joseph William, and John Spooner were all raised Masters. William Clarke, an inn-holder, one of the brethren named, it appears, was ballotted for in June, 1766, and probably was made the next lodge night, but there is, unfortunately, a hiatus between June, 1766, and December, 1767, through the destructiveness of the juveniles who have had access to, and done their best to maltreat, this old record of the British Union.

In December, 1767, there is the usual record of the election of the Master and Wardens, with the addition of that of Secretary, Bro. John Spooner being appointed to that responsible office. At this lodge, William Kerridge was made a Mason in due form, " agreeable to ye order of last lodge night, having paid one guinea in ye hands of Mr. John Prentice for his admission." A similar memorandum is made against several names of brethren made, and we are, therefore, left to the conclusion, as before suggested, that a guinea was the fee charged for initiation, and that it included admission to the fellowcraft degree, but whether it also carried the candidate through the third degree is not made manifest. Certain it is that the fee charged was very much less than at present. Mr. Robert Easter, of Walton-on-the-Naze, was ballotted for, and duly elected, made an entered apprentice, and " past " fellowcraft, July 21st, 1768. This is the first record of the word *passed* as applied to the F.C. degree.

At the regular meeting on the 20th February, 1769, we find that Bro. William Kerridge *was proposed to be raised Master* next lodge night (he was subsequently made M.M. in April), from which it would appear that brethren did not as a matter of right go forward to the third degree, but were, in some measure, dependent upon the goodwill of the lodge, and we will suppose their own merits, for advancement in the order. Kerridge had been made in May, 1768.

From an entry made in the minute book it would appear that the meeting on the 20th March, 1769, was held at the Green Man, a hostelry which probably at that time held a much better position than it does now, as it is a very humble tavern. At the next meeting, held on the 3rd April, in the same year, the following important note occurs:

"At this lodge it was agreed that the incorporating the Society of Free and Accepted Masons would be of general benefit, and past this lodge *nemine contradicente*, and the instrument for that purpose was signed accordingly."

The Freemasons as a society have never been incorporated yet, except, I understand, the Supreme Council of the 33°, A. & A. Rite, which, I believe, was registered two or three years since. In 1771, a bill was brought into Parliament by the Honourable Charles Dillon, the Deputy Grand Master, for incorporating the Society by Act of Parliament; but on the second reading of the bill, it having been opposed by Mr. Onslow, at the desire of several brethren who had petitioned the House against it, Mr. Dillon moved to postpone the consideration of it "sine die," thus the design of an incorporation fell to the ground. There are some who still think, however, amongst the number, that the resolution of the members of the British Union was a good one, and the incorporation of the Craft "a consummation devoutly to be wished.

Two brethren, visitors from the Royal Alfred Lodge, attended the lodge meeting in September, 1770. Bro. Joseph Clarke was duly elected R.W.M. on the 27th December, 1770. The Wardens and Secretary were also elected, as appears to have been customary at this period.

William Barnes was made a Mason March 29, 1771, and raised to the degree of F.C., and in August of that year Mark Lione was made.

At this date, we note that Bro. Wootton has received £2 7s. to be accounted for:—

For Bro. Woollaston	£1	1 0
For Bro. Marks Lione	1	6 0
	£2	7 0

Bro. Woollaston is entered before as Woolverston and Woollaston indifferently, and appears to have been made in August, 1770. Let us hope that Bro. Lione was not a *foreigner*, and charged higher than a native would have been for the honours of Masonry. Such things have been, and at the present time there is a wide distinction between a foreigner, or one born without the pale of Ipswich and Suffolk, and a man "native, and to the manner born," though it is fair to add that this exclusiveness does not extend to Masons and Masonry so far as my experience goes. *

In September, 1771, one Thomas Milner was proposed and "legally admitted"; appended is a note to the effect that the above Thomas Milner was afterwards rejected, being a Minor.

Marks Lione was *raised* fellow craft 16th September, 1771, which appears to be the first instance on record of a brother being passed at an interval of time after his being admitted.

December 28th, 1771, St. John's. At a lodge then held Bro. John Prentice was elected Right Worshipful Master. So runs the minute of that day. The Wardens, Secretary, and Tyler, were all elected at the same time. On the 4th January, 1773, I find it ordered that no person be in future made a brother of this Lodge for a less consideration than the sum of £1 11s. 6d.

Touching this said term, Right Worshipful, I have already

---

* See Mrs. Ellvert — "A Woman' Wrongs", "St. Bede," &c., for the opinion of a literateur on the exercise of hospitality, and the kindness to strangers shown by the East Anglians, or the reverse.

said, it is the style of a Knight, though the old heralds say that Esquire is also a title of Worship. By the way, if I mistake not, the members of the Royal Order of Scotland (who are said to have descended from the Knights, whom Robert the Bruce erected into a new order of Masonic chivalry after the battle of Bannockburn in 1314), address each other formally as Right Worshipful Sir, and claim to be Knights Companions of the R.S.Y.C.S.

Old Izaak Walton, who is just now denounced by some of the Faculty as the most thorough-going vivisector in his following the "gentle craft," dedicates his world-known book, "The Complete Angler," to the Right Worshipful John Offley, Esq., of Madeley Manor, in the county of Stafford; "My most honoured Friend." The date of the work is 1653.

Can any one tell us if Walton was a Freemason? He speaks of "my friend Elias Ashmole, Esq.," who all the world knows was a member of the Craft and a Rosicrucian, and it would be interesting to know whether he himself was one of the little band of Speculative Masons who kept the Craft alive at that time.

To return to the British Union and its Records, between December 1771 and January, 1773, only one meeting appears to have been held, and no record seems to have been regularly made from this time, of the absent as well as present members as heretofore, and consequently no clue given as to the prosperity and numbers of the Lodge. In July, 1762, there appear to have been eleven members in the Lodge, three of whom were absent. In February, 1769, there must have been fourteen members, eight of whom are written off as absent, two being at sea, and another excused. At the November meeting in 1769, held at the Green Man, six were present besides two visitors, and eight were absent. Old Ipswich and Suffolk names constantly appear—Clarke, Prentice, Fenn, Dodd, Oliver, Harris, Bailey, Woollaston, or Wollaston, Whiteside, Woodward, Kerridge, Tovell, and others being amongst the number.

Under date 17th November, 1773, we find the following:—
"At this Lodge a letter from Rowland Holt, Esq., Prov. Grand Master for the County of Suffolk, was read, and it was agreed and ordered that the Master of this Lodge do answer the same by the next general post, and that he wait on the Grand Secretary, and subscribe one guinea towards the general charity, to be paid out of this Lodge."

In January, 1774, we find that Thomas Milner, who had been previously rejected as a Minor, was now "made in due form and raised fellow craft." It was agreed and ordered that the sum of three shillings be paid into the hands of the Treasurer by every Brother belonging to the Lodge; no more than the sum of one shilling being spent on every lodge night for each member then present, the remainder to be applied as a fund for such purposes as the Lodge should think fit. Eleven Brethren were present on this occasion, and four noted as absent. On the 27th December, 1774, we find the following note:—

"At the above Lodge held this day, John Spooner was chose (sic) S.W. in the room of Bro. R. Tovell, and after was chose R.W.M.; W. Paxman, S.W.; John Prentice, J.W.; W. Usher, Tyler; Robert Manning, Secretary; Peter Wotton, Treasurer."

It would seem from this note, that the Brethren thought it necessary that a Brother should fill the office of S.W. previous to his election to the chair of K.S., but the Book of Constitutions merely directs that a Master shall have filled the office of Warden (either Senior or Junior is sufficient to render a candidate eligible) for twelve calendar months. A very salutary regulation.

In January, 1775, James Woollward and Robert Manning were raised to the degree of Master, and paid to Peter Wootton, Treasurer, five shillings each.

It would appear from this, that an extra and special charge was made for this degree a century ago. What would our Brethren say if such were the practice now? Woollward had been made August, 1770, and Manning January, 1774; so it is clear that at this time it was customary for a much longer period to elapse between the conferring of the second and third degrees than is at present practised. On the other hand a much shorter interval occurred between the first and second degrees, which were, in fact, mostly given the same night. Our present system, which keeps the mean between the two extremes (as the Preface to our good old Prayer Book says), seems, after all, the best; a month's interval between each degree being, to my thinking, much better than the Scotch rule, which allows all the degrees to be given at one Lodge on one night; or the Prussian, which requires an interval of a year between each degree. On the 1st February, 1775, we find it resolved that the Lodge do remit to the Grand Fund of Charity £1 1s., *also the sum of four shillings towards the building of the Hall!*

At this time, Lord Petre, a Roman Catholic, was Grand Master, and under his auspices Freemasons' Hall was commenced and completed. The Committee formed for that purpose purchased the ground in Gt. Queen Street, and the conveyance of the premises was made out in the names of Lord Petre, the Dukes of Beaufort and Chandos, Earl Ferrers, and Viscount Dudley and Ward, who were appointed Trustees. In 1792, £20,000 had been expended on the building, and if other Lodges contributed as liberally as the British Union, we can understand readily the statement made by Preston, that a considerable debt remained on the building. On the 1st February, 1775, we find a note which, I will answer for it, will not be found in the Minutes of this year of grace, 1875.

"Received of the visiting Brethren, 5s."

Whatever was the case a century ago, the Members of the British Union of to-day pride themselves on the exercise of a courteous reception to all and sundry, and evidence in their conduct their full belief in the sacred rites of hospitality. May the day be long distant when visitors are otherwise received, and when the stranger is expected to pay for all he gets.

At a Special Lodge held at the Green Man, 28th April, 1775, it was agreed and ordered that " from this night forward, every Brother belonging to this Lodge, shall meet on the first Tuesday of every month and spend one shilling, or being absent forfeit as undermentioned, and the forfeits to be expended once a quarter of a year, and whatever Brother shall not pay off his arrears once a quarter to be excluded—viz.,

R.W.M. ... ... 2s. 0d.

S. & J. Wardens ... 1s. 6d.

Any other of the Brethren one shilling on not showing sufficient cause of such absence."

Nine Brethren were present at this meeting and four are recorded as absent.

Would it not be a good thing to revive these fines in some of our Lodges where there is too often a lax attendance on the part of the officers?

The Lodge seems flourishing at this time, for at the May meeting in 1776, held on the 7th, we find twelve members present, nine absent, and two candidates were admitted to the first and second degrees.

A Lodge appears to have been held on the following night, a most unusual course, and, if an adjourned meeting, I believe unconstitutional. At this Lodge, Benjamin Woollward and Edward Wiles were raised Masters, and paid five shillings each. Miles was Tyler, and had been initiated and passed February, 1775,

We find another most interesting note at this meeting, as follows:—

" By order of the Lodge the Treasurer paid Bro. Pargman and Bro. Prentice four shillings each, as Operative Masons."

The November Lodge in this year was well attended: eighteen members were present, eleven visitors, and four are recorded as absent. William Woollaston, John Bloomfield, John Humphreys, and Robert Bowles (all Ipswich names) were *raised* to the degree of fellow craft on this occasion, two of these brethren having been made in September.

They must have been a genial lot, these brethren of a century since, for, at the next Lodge, held on the 15th November, we find a note to the effect that, " This night the above members went in procession to the play, called ' Bold Stroke for a Wife, with the Padlock.' Had a full house."

One fancies that, as with the outside world, sometimes all is not so serene as it should be in Masonry, for at the Lodge held on St. John's Day, 27th December, 1776, at the Green Man, we find the following:—

" Bro. James Woollward, S.W. by seniority, was to have taken the chair, but as Wm. Clarke, R.W.M., was absent, all business (particularly that on St. John's Day) was omitted; also Bro. Manning, J.W., insisted on resigning the jewel, on account of the Lodge not being regularly kept up."

Bro. Woollward either was not competent, or he was not popular, for we find that at the March meeting in 1777, Robert Manning was elected R.W.M.; John Prentice, S.W.; Benj. Foxwell, J.W.; J. Bloomfield, Treasurer and Secretary; and Bro. Paxman, Tyler, for the remainder of the year.

" Resolved this night that every brother who intends to belong to this Lodge, shall sign his hand and pay into the hands of the Treasurer the sum of three shillings as quarterage, and so on for every quarter. Upon default thereof, his name is to be erased from the Lodge.

Here follows the list of members, and for the benefit of the Ipswich and Suffolk readers of these "Masonic Papers," some of whose ancestors may be amongst them, I will give the names:—

Joseph Clarke; W. Clarke; Robert Manning, R.W.M.; John Prentice, S.W.; Edward Wiles; Wm. Prentice; Benj. Woollard; Wm. Howes; Lawrence Rainbird; John Humphries; Charles Lord; Edmund Prentice; John Philby; Cornelius Hill; Samuel Ribbans; Benj. Huggins; R. Page, Junr.; John Blomfield, Treasurer and Secretary; Benj. Foxwell, J.W.; Wm. Usher; Wm. Kerridge; Robert King; John Spooner; James Woollward; Caleb Howard. On the 10th March, 1777, Bros. Huggins, Blomfield, Humphreys, Usher, E. Prentice, C. Hill, and another Brother whose name is indecipherable, were raised to the degree of Master, and for the cash account for that evening, we find the entry: seven Brothers, raised Masters, £2 odd. The shillings and pence are torn off, which is perhaps as well, since the next entry is also wanting the amount "*received from two visiting brethren*"—pointing to a very objectionable and most unhospitable practice noticed before, of making the visitors pay for whatever they got.

Under date May 6th, 1777, I find the following entry:—" By order of the Grand Lodge no person shall be made a Mason for less than £2 2s., and made a resolve of this Lodge accordingly."

The Green Man seems to have become unpopular to the Brethren of the Lodge. Probably as the Grand Lodge had raised the fee for initiation, candidates of a higher class were seeking admission, and the humble hostelry which had been deemed good enough for the founders of the Lodge and their immediate successors, was now considered not sufficiently aristocratic for the Brethren introduced under the new *régime*. At any rate, on the

3rd June, 1777, a motion was made by the R.W.M., at the request of several Brethren, to have the Lodge removed, and it was ballotted for accordingly, when the members voted—

    For its removal 10
    Against 3

It was therefore agreed "That this Lodge be removed to Bro. Philby's, at the Coffee House in Ipswich, if the Deputy Grand Master thinks proper."

On the 8th July, the Lodge, still meeting at the Green Man, Godfrey Burdett was proposed, and he was made and passed a fellowcraft at the August meeting. Up to this time the Lodge had no name; but on the 29th July, 1777, we find a very important and very interesting minute. It runs as follows:—
" From this evening 'tis resolved this Lodge is called by the title of the British Union Lodge, Ipswich, and ordered to be inserted in the Grand List of Lodges accordingly."

On the 2nd September, we find the Lodge had removed to the Coffee House, and Bro. J. Philby proposed that night General Green as a candidate for Masonic honours, and at the following Lodge meeting in October, the gallant officer and William Lane "were made Masons, and admitted to the degree of fellows of the craft."

On the 4th November, we come across another entry, which will be of interest to the present members of the Lodge, since some of the old jewels are still in use :—

"To Bro. John Prentice for P.M. Jewel, seventeen shillings, paid by the Treasurer, also to Bro. Spooner for the Secretary's Jewel and the P.M. ribband nineteen shillings, paid also by the Treasurer; and that the said jewels are now the property of the said Lodge."

On the 13th November, Bros. Lord, Philby, Burdett, Drake, Green, and Land, were raised to the degree of Master, and paid the sum of five shillings each, and one shilling each to the Tyler. Either the ceremony must have been much shorter than it is now, or the brethren must have been taken all together, for it would be impossible to go through the ceremony with each separately, as is now generally the practice in working this sublime degree. In this night's cash account, we find " To Bro. Prentice, for the book of the History of Masonry, 3s."

One would be anxious to know what history this was, who it was by, and where the copy now is.

On the 21st December, the Brethren went to the play to see the "Merry Wives of Windsor," by our *Brother* Shakespeare, as our excellent Bro. Parkinson would say. Twenty members and twelve visitors, including one clergyman, the Rev. Drake (as they say in Suffolk), appear to have been present, and eight are entered as absent. The Lodge appears to have flourished at this time. Removing to Bro. Philby's Coffee House had probably raised it in public estimation, hence the influx of new members. On the 2nd of December the thanks of the Lodge were given to Bro. Philby for a present of a set of jewels and working tools.

On the 27th December, 1777, fifteen members were present, and being the Festival of St. John, the Officers were elected. The minute is thus recorded :—

" The Brotherhood elect Bro. Joseph Clarke Master of this Lodge for 1778; Bro. Benj. Foxwell, S.W., and Bro. J. Blomfield, J.W. for the said year. Also Bro. Wm. Drake, Secretary and Treasurer. Also that the Lodge do present to Bro. John Blomfield, late Secretary and Treasurer, a medal for his indefatigable services in his late office."

Under date January 6th, 1778, I find a long array of names of Brethren of the Lodge, though we can hardly imagine them all to have been present. No less than forty-two are entered, amongst them we note many well-known Ipswich names: Churchman, Gooding, King, Canham, Popper, Catchpole, Crisp, Sparrow, Spalding, Garrett, Toosey, Elliston, Deward, and Mills being amongst the number. The Lodge this night bought a new Book of Constitutions, price 10s. 6d., rather a high figure for the work. On **February 24th**, Thomas Askew and Wm. Christie were regularly made and admitted fellowcrafts. Both are Ipswich names, and no doubt relatives of both are living, though I fancy they are not now Masons.

At the May meeting it was resolved that the yearly subscription should be twelve shillings.

At the end of this first volume of the minutes, I find a debtor and creditor account of the Lodge, from which it appears that Bro. Joseph Clarke, who was made March 8th, 1762, and paid £1 11s. 6d. for his initiation, and the subsequently made Masons paid £1 1s. One Brother hailed from Sunderland, the majority were from Harwich, and one was a Yarmouth man.

At the June meeting in 1778, twenty-five were present, so the Lodge must have been flourishing then.

Under date September 1st, 1778, by the unanimous consent of the Lodge, Bro. R—— H—— was rejected becoming a member of this Lodge. One would like to know how Mr. H. had so raised the ire of this Lodge as to ensure his unanimous rejection.

The first minute book of this old Lodge ends in 1779, with a list of the members of the British Union which would have been interesting if it were complete, but unfortunately half the sheet containing the names is torn out, and as a large number of the pages are maltreated in the same way, it is possible that many important minutes are irrecoverably lost.

SECOND MINUTE BOOK.

THE second Minute Book of this old Lodge commences 1779, with a cash account—and disbursements on the 27th December,

St. John's Day—from which it appears that the banquet was at the expense of the Lodge; a very bad custom, and one it would be well not to see imitated, though I fear amongst the London Lodges it is in many cases the rule, and not the exception, that the Brethren dine at the expense of the Lodge, and not at their own, and the great Masonic charities suffer in consequence.

On this night I find amongst the payments:—" To meat and sauce for dinner," £1 19s. 6d.; for liquor, £2 4s.; total £4 3s. 6d.—for eating and drinking! and below it is ordered that the Treasurer do send to Bro. Heseltine, Grand Secretary, *one guinea* for the use of the General Fund of Charity, by February 1st, 1780.

Here is a text for a Masonic sermon at once. The Brethren of the British Union Lodge of to-day (except in the laudable exercise of hospitality, always exercised without stint or measure, to all visitors, no matter from whence they come, who honour the Lodge by their presence at its meetings), never allow the funds of the Lodge to be expended in refreshment, as so many metropolitan Lodges do, but each member pays a reasonable price, say two shillings and sixpence, for a thoroughly substantial, but by no means extravagant, repast, and he may take what stimulant he pleases, or none at all, so that if he is a teetotaler, and even a Good Templar, he is perfectly at liberty to drink his toasts in water if he please, no man urging him to drink or to abstain, but leaving him to do what seems best in his own eyes.

One of the great objections to Masonry I have seen somewhere, has been its suppers and its toasts, inciting men to drink against their will, and leading weak men astray, by the gay society of the craft. For myself, I do not believe for a moment in the statements made by our enemies, that Masonry or its banquets have a tendency to lead men astray.

I strongly believe in the social part of the Masonic meeting, when the brethren from labour seek refreshment, and I should be sorry to see the pleasant after part done away with, but at the same time I am strongly of opinion that the Lodge funds should never be trenched upon except in exercise of hospitality to strangers; but the members who stay to supper, or dinner, or whatever name it goes by, should be content to pay for it. Were this practice universal, and extravagant banquets tabooed, the charities would get the benefit, and the social gatherings would be none the less pleasant because they were inexpensive. This is a matter which chiefly concerns our London brethren, however, as, except in Liverpool perhaps, and one or two of our great cities the provincial Masons do not go in for extravagant banquets, save on very rare occasions. Even at our Provincial Grand Lodge meetings, the dinner provided is generally a question of a few shillings only, and I do not know that when properly served (which by the way is seldom the case, through the great paucity of waiters), they are not as pleasant as the monthly and quarterly banquets held by some London Lodges at a cost of a guinea, and sometimes two, to each brother who wishes to partake of the costly repast.

Apparently harmony did not reign supreme in the British Union at this time, for on the 7th March, 1780, we find a record that "Bro. T. C—— (for obvious reasons we suppress the names), by order of the Master and the rest of the brethren, is excluded this Lodge;" the reason of his exclusion is carefully scored out, and no one but an expert, or the celebrated Blind Man at the Post Office, could now decipher the cause of this order. Likewise W. K——, for a scandalous report of calling the fraternity a —— society, and that advice be sent to the Grand Lodge, in order to have him erased out of their book, and excluded from all regular Lodges," &c. So runs the minute, and from it we cannot fail to gather that the Lodge (as too many Lodges are now doing every day) had made the great mistake of admitting men within its portals who would do nothing but bring the society into contempt, so thoroughly and manifestly unfit were they to participate in the mysteries of Masonry.

On the 5th June, 1781, we note the following minute, which is suggestive in many ways:—

"This evening it was unanimously agreed that the Secretary should provide the Lodge with a Freemasons' Calendar annually, and the expense to be paid out of the fund of the Lodge." One cannot help thinking we should have more masonic students, more seekers after light, and fewer knife and fork Masons, if each Lodge now took, not only the *Cosmopolitan Masonic Calendar*, but the *Freemason*, and the *Masonic Magazine*, and so contributed to the diffusion of masonic knowledge, and to what is of so great value in these days of calumny and calling in question, the collection and preservation of masonic facts.

To return to the minutes, I have here to note that the information is of the most meagre description, the account of each Lodge meeting contains little more than a list of names of those present, and now and then a cash account, from which I gather that all refreshment supplied was at the expense of the Lodge funds, except in the case of a visitor, who was generally mulcted of eighteenpence for what he took.

In September, 1781, the Lodge was removed to Bro. S. Ribbans', at the "Golden Lion," then, as now, a famous hostelry; and, on the following Lodge night, it was ordered, "that the Secretary do send to the Grand Lodge to acquaint them of the same immediately, to have their approbation." It would appear that the Provincial Grand Master was never consulted in the matter. At the present time it is doubtful whether a step of this kind would be allowed without the sanction of the Prov. G.M.

At the lodge held in June, 1782, we note the presence of a

visiting brother, Andrew Gough, from the United Traders' Lodge, "Pewter Platter," Hart Street, Covent Garden.

On the 24th June, St. John Baptist's day, we find that the festival was duly kept, and apparently at the expense of the Lodge, for under the head of disbursements, we notice the significant items, Bill, £2 17s. 10d.; servants, 5s. Eleven brethren were present.

On the 30th June, we find the following interesting minute:— "This evening Mr. Wm. Lane, operative mason, was made in due forme, and raised (sic) to ye second degree, and paid his admission money into the hands of the Treasurer, and one pound one shilling for the expense of the evening."

The admission fee at the time appears to have been £2 2s., besides a registration fee of 8s. 6d, and this only took the brother into the second degree.

There could hardly have been any settled fee, however, after initiation, for I find Bro. Philby charged 8s. 6d. for the second and third degrees, which were both given to him on one night, the 2nd October, 1781; and, on the same occasion, Bro. John Covenoy, a visiting Brother, was raised a Master Mason, and charged 10s. 6d. for the degree. On the occasion of Bro. Lane's being initiated, he is charged £2 2s., besides 8s. 6d. registration fee, and an extra 2s. 6d. for being *raised* to the second degree, so that with the amount charged "for the expense of the evening," the operative mason pays altogether £3 14s., which only takes him through the second degree.

Let us hope he was a well-to-do operative, or he would not have much encouragement to proceed further, from the fees and fines exacted.

By the way, it has always struck me that it is a great pity Grand Lodge does not encourage the admission of operative masons, and the formation of operative Lodges, pure and simple, where the principles of architecture, and the mysteries of building might be taught. In Scotland, some of the ancient operative Lodges still exist, and speculative masonry is still connected with its originator, operative masonry, much, I trust, to their mutual advantage. At present, so far as we know, there is no connection between the Craft and the architects and builders of to-day,—more's the pity, at least so far as England is concerned.

In the Antient and Accepted Rite there is a degree, the twelfth of that Rite, and the ninth of the Ineffable series, known as Grand Master Architect, which presupposes a connection with operative masonry, and of which we find the following account in *Webb's Freemason's Monitor*, an American work of some reputation:—" This is strictly speaking a scientific degree, and much resembles in this respect the second or fellowcraft degree of the York Rite. In it the principles of architecture, and the connection of the liberal arts and sciences with masonry are unfolded, and the lecture embraces a series of instructions well calculated to interest the neophyte. The candidate for admission is subjected to a rigid examination as to his skill and proficiency in architecture (masonry), and is required to produce evidence that he is qualified intellectually and morally to be admitted among the G.M.A., and engage in building the great moral edifice. The assembly is called a Chapter. It is decorated with white hangings, sprinkled with red flames, emblematical of the purity of heart, and zeal, which should be the characteristics of every G.M.A. The five arches of architecture should be delineated in the Chapter, together with a representation of the north star in the north, and seven small stars surrounding it. This signifies that as the north star is a sure guide to mariners, so should virtue be the guiding star of every G.M.A. The Master, seated in the E., represents King Solomon; he is styled Most Potent. The S.W., in the W., is called Grand Inspector. The brethren, in addition to black robes and capes, as in the preceding degree, wear a stone-coloured ribbon from the left shoulder to the right hip, like the Royal Arch sash, and the jewel is suspended from it as in the Royal Order of Scotland. The jewel is a gold medal with the five orders of architecture, a star, and a case of mathematical instruments delineated on both sides. The apron is of stone colour, with a pocket in the centre, and on the flap a star." Mackey says the apron is white, lined and bordered with black, with a compass, square, and rule painted thereon. The French have the same colour, but do not mention the compass, square, and rule. The following is the symbolic history, for the truth of which I need hardly say I do not vouch. "Masonic tradition (according to Bro. Carson's Monitor of the Antient and Accepted Rite) informs us that King S. established this grade with a view to forming a school of architecture, for the instruction of the craftsmen employed in the building of the Temple, and to animate them with a desire of arriving at perfection in the royal art. He was a prince equally renowned for his justice, wisdom, and foresight: he, therefore, desired to reward the faithful and meritorious craftsmen; so that by perfection in the art, they might be better prepared to approach the throne of God. He accordingly, for this purpose, cast his eyes upon the Grand Masters of the workmen, the Sublime Knights Elected, as persons properly qualified to assist him in preparing for the fulfilment of the promise made to Enoch, to Moses, and to David, that in the fulness of time God would dwell in a fixed Temple, and that His name should be there."

Mackey, in his admirable *Lexicon of Masonry*, to which I have alluded before in the course of these notes, tells us of another degree connected with architecture, and it must be admitted with the occult sciences, in the order of African Architects. It appears that in the year 1767, one Baucherren instituted in Prussia, with the concurrence of Frederick II., a society which he called by the above name. The object of the Institution was historical research; but it contained a Ritual which partook of masonry, Christianity, alchemy, and chivalry. It was divided into two temples, and was composed of eleven degrees. In the first temple were the degrees of 1, Apprentice; 2, Fellowcraft; and 3, Master. In the second temple were the degrees of 4, Apprentice of Egyptian Secrets; 5, Initiate of Egyptian Secrets; 6, Cosmopolitan Brother; 7, Christian Philosopher; 8, Master of Egyptian Secrets; 9, Esquire; 10, Soldier; and 11, Knight. The Society constructed a vast building intended as a Grand Chapter of the Order, and which contained an excellent library, a museum of natural history, and a chemical laboratory. For a long time the African Architects decreed annually a gold medal, worth fifty ducats, to the author of the best memoir on the history of masonry. Why should not the Grand Lodge, or the Supreme Council, do the same?

Ragon, who seldom speaks well of any other rite than his own, has, however, in his *Orthodoxie Maçonnique*, paid the following tribute to the African Architects:—" Their intercourse was modest and dignified. They did not esteem decorations, aprons, collars, jewels, &c., but were rather fond of luxury, and delighted in sententious apothegms, whose meaning was sublime, but concealed. In their assemblies they read essays, and communicated the results of their researches. At their simple and decorous banquets instructive and scientific discourses were delivered. While their initiations were gratuitous, they gave liberal assistance to such zealous brethren as were in needy circumstances. They published in Germany many important documents on the subject of Freemasonry."

Under date, October 3, 1782, we find that this evening a Lodge was convened by order of the R.W.M. and Wardens in order to "spend ye evening with Bro. John Blomfield, and from him to receive the benefit of the 3 L......s, which was accordingly done to ye general satisfaction of the brethren present."

No doubt Bro. Bloomfield delivered or explained the three lectures, and it is noteworthy the guarded way in which this is noted, very different to the open and diffuse manner in which the minutes are often kept, and perhaps, I might add, too often reported in the *Freemason*.

On St. John the Evangelist's Day, December 27, 1782, it is recorded that this evening Bro. Robert Tovell, Secretary, was raised to the degree of Past Master, being found worthy.

Some of our younger brethren will be surprised to learn that it was a common custom in the last century, and is, I believe, even now, in Scotland, to confer the titular degree of Past Master upon brethren who have never passed the chair. In England now we all know a Past Master is a brother who has served the office of Warden in some warranted lodge, and has been elected by the majority of the lodge to fill the chair of K.S. He is then duly installed, receiving the secrets of what are called the Installed Master's degree, and from thenceforth, so long as he is a subscribing member of any lodge, he retains his rank as Past Master and is entitled to a seat in Grand Lodge.

On the 5th November, 1782, "Mr. John Spooner was nominated to take the chair for the ensuing year; and at the St. John's Festival following he was elected R.W.M.; Bro. B. Foxwell, S.W.; Bro. Jacob Bunnett, J.W.; Bro. S. Ribbans, Treasurer; and Robert Tovell, Secretary. Thus it would appear, as has been before remarked, that at this time all the superior officers in the lodge were elected, as is the case now in Royal Arch Chapters, and not as now, when the W.M. appoints all his own officers from the S.W. downwards, except the Treasurer, who keeps the keys of the money-chest, and the Tyler, who is the serving brother of the Lodge, and not the servant of the Master, as some appear to think.

On March 4th, 1783, Robert Koymer, from " ye Twins Lodge, Norwich," was a visitor. No such Lodge appears now in the "Cosmopolitan Calendar," though there are no less than six in the old cathedral town.

William Lane, Operative Mason, appears amongst the brethren present at a Lodge holden on the 4th November, 1783, and I find that on this evening the brethren went from the Lodge room at ye Golden Lyon in procession to the theatre to see the comedy, "As You Like It," with the musical piece called the "Deserter." The same evening Michael Sharp, musician; Peter Dagueville, dancing master; Thomas Smith, innholder; Stephen Prentice, shipwright; and William Bennett, cooper and innholder, were proposed for initiation.

On November 18, 1783, " Bro. James Garrod was raised to ye degree of Master Mason, being found worthy." This night also " Mr. M. Sharp was made a Mason in due form, and was admitted to the second and third degree of Masonry." The other four brethren noted above were all initiated, but took only the first degree. This is the first instance we have yet come across where a brother has taken the three degrees in one night. The fees are all given, and it appears Bro. Sharp was charged as follows:—

For Admission	...	...	£2 2 0
,, Registration Fees		...	0 8 6
,, Second Degree	...	...	0 2 6
,, Raised Master	...	...	0 6 0
			£2 19 0

There were eight visitors present, and seven of them appear to have paid ten shillings and sixpence altogether for the honour of sitting at the same table with the brethren of the British Union.

Under date January 6, 1784, I note that this evening, "R. L. (of course I do not publish the name) was expelled this Lodge for unworthy transactions perfectly clear to ye R.W.M. and brethren then present, and was in due form divested of the badge of a Mason by the J.W."

On March 2, 1784, I note that whilst Bro. Bennett was raised to ye degree of a Master Mason, Bros. T. Askew, Thomas Smith, and G. Walham " passed ye chair." This, of course, alludes to the titular Past Master degree, of which mention has already been made. Two brethren—one a grocer, and the other a cabinet maker—were initiated on the 14th June, 1784.

On the 24th of that month, St. John Baptist's Day, the brethren went in procession to St. Mary Tower Church, and an excellent sermon was preached from the 20th and 21st verses of St. Jude by the Rev. V. L. Barnard, who afterwards visited the Lodge in October. Several brethren from Hadleigh were proposed to take the second and third degrees the following lodge night. Under the head of disbursements for this night we find: To one dozen aprons, this day, 12s. What would my good friend Bro. Keuning say to such a price for aprons now-a-days? I am afraid they must have been poor lambskins, or else the price of leather has strangely gone up since 1784.

At the lodge meeting, November 2, 1784, it was proposed that Bros. J. Gooding, W. Harris, and Thomas Smith should be passed and raised to third degree next lodge night; so that, as we have before remarked, it is evident that at this time brethren did not take their degrees as a matter of course as they do now, but each step was taken by favour of the Lodge.

Bro. William Lane, operative Mason, became S.W. this year, being elected 27th December, St. John's Day, when the festival was duly observed, and the brethren had an ordinary at one shilling and sixpence, dinner being ordered for twenty, and at the Lodge there appear to have been present a deputation from the Lodge No. 426 in ye King's 1st Regiment of Dragoon Guards, which was probably quartered in the town at that time, the brethren representing this military Lodge consisting of the D.R.W.M., a P.M., and the S. and J.W.'s.

I note that there was paid to Bro. Foxwell 3s. for painting and gilding ye flag-staff belonging to ye Royal Edmund Lodge; but what this Lodge was, whether it is still in existence, and why the British Union had to pay, I cannot tell.

The Lodge meeting on January 27, 1785, was convened at Bro. Higgin's, at ye Bull, Cornhill, Ipswich. Why it met here, and whether there was authority to do so, does not appear. "This evening it was unanimously agreed that no Mason who is not a member of any Lodge, and being a resident of this town, shall not be allowed to visit this Lodge any more than three times, except they choose to join and make proofs of their being a subscriber of some constituted Lodge." The English is a little defective, but the meaning is obvious, which reminds me of a reply Coleridge made to some lady's argument, " Madam, your reasons are wrong, but your conclusious are right."

Some people think that when people are proposed as Freemasons, as a matter of course they are accepted—free and accepted—the brethren being only too eager to take anybody in. Whatever may be the fact now in some lodges, it was not so in 1785 in the British Union, for I find that on the 1st March of that year, Mr. L. P. (I think it better not to give the name) was ballotted for and rejected, and his admission money was returned to the brother who proposed him, which brother and another in consequence, I suppose, of his rejection, thereupon withdrew themselves from the Lodge.

On May 30, 1785, a Lodge was convened, " in order to inform Bro. John Conder, Bro. M. Willoughby, and Bro. W. Fenton of a dispensation being sent for them to hold a Lodge of Free and Accepted Masons in due form at the Green Man, Ipswich, for the space of six months and no longer. Signed and sealed by Rowland Holt, Esq., Prov. Gr. Master for Suffolk."

At the August meeting, in 1785, three brethren from the Perfect Friendship Lodge were present as visitors. It was ordered and agreed to this evening by the R.W.M. and brethren present, that any visiting brother from ye Lodge of Perfect Friendship should pay no more than one shilling for each visit to this Lodge; and it is also agreed by the R.W.M. and brethren of the Lodge of Perfect Friendship that no brother from the British Union Lodge shall pay any more than one shilling for each visit to them. So a treaty of reciprocity appears to have been entered into, and the most favoured country clause of modern commercial treaties anticipated. At the following meeting it was " ordered and agreed that if any brother chooses to eat supper he must pay that expense extraordinary, as no eating is allowed to be paid for out of the fund of the Lodge. N.B.—the above is ordered to be made the 25th article in ye code of by-laws." This was an excellent rule, and one that should be universally adopted, but it would have been better had it extended to the drinking as well as eating. Bro. William Lane was elected December, 1785, as R.W.M., and Mr. John Morgan, surgeon, was proposed for initiation, and on the following Lodge night the quarterage was raised from three shillings to four shillings. In February, Mr. Hugh Dyer, an operative Mason, was proposed for initiation, and was initiated in March. Under the head of disbursements we note—" Relieved a stranger, two shillings and sixpence. N.B.—the above stranger called himself Abraham Shrrief, an Algerine." At the June meeting we note, to a distressed brother two shil-

lings and sixpence; and in the August following another note—
to a stranger two shillings and sixpence.

At the November meeting, in 1786, we find the following minute:—" This evening it was ordered by the R.W.M. and brethren present that ye Secretary do write to Bro. Blomfield to inquire into ye merits of nominating a gentleman in the county to preside as Prov. Gr. Master to fill ye vacancy of R. Holt, Esq., deceased. N.B.—the gentlemen mentioned are P.C. Crespigny, Esq., William Middleton, Esq., and — Holt, Esq." The William Middleton here mentioned was no doubt the same gentleman mentioned in Burke as of Crowfield Hall. He was the son of Arthur Middleton, Governor of South Carolina, and his eldest son, who by the way appears to have been born this year (1786), was created a Baronet in 1804. He married the sister of Earl Brownlow. The present representative of the family is Admiral Sir George Brooke-Middleton; and Shrublands, the family seat, is one of the finest places in Suffolk. The P. C. Crespigny mentioned was probably the Philip Champion de Crespigny, who was M P. for Aldeburgh, Suffolk, and died in 1803. It was his brother who was created a baronet in 1805, he having received the Prince Regent at his place in Surrey. He was Receiver-General of Droits of Admiralty for half a century, and his son, the second baronet, who was M P. for Southampton, and married the daughter of the fourth Earl of Plymouth, was Provincial Grand Master of Hants. The De Crespignys are of French extraction, and claim to descend from the Barons de Frênes and Viscomte de Vire, who flourished about 1350. There is little doubt but that either of these gentlemen would have dignified the office of Prov. Grand Master for Suffolk.

The second minute book of the British Union Lodge terminates with this record.

I have alluded to the introduction of operative Masons into

our Order as testified in these records, and I am disposed to suggest, that Grand Lodge, the Supreme Council 33°, and Grand Mark Lodge especially, as being perhaps most nearly allied to operative Masonry, should foster the study of architecture in every way. Why should they not, for instance, give a gold medal away every year to the writer of the best paper on architecture or archæology, or any kindred subject, or for the best design for cathedral, church, castle, or mansion? Would it not be a good thing if operative Masons were encouraged to join us by being admitted at a lower fee, and in the case of the A. and A. Rite I believe it would popularise that Rite and make it much more useful if all architects were given up to the 12th degree, that of Grand Master Architect, for a nominal fee on taking the usual obligation of allegiance to the S.G.C. 33°. Further we submit that such offices as Grand and Prov. Grand Superintendent of Works in the Craft, and Grand Inspector of Works in the Mark Grand Lodge should be confined exclusively to professional architects or civil engineers, or to such as have made architecture and archæology their peculiar study. I have known drapers appointed to such offices who did not know what archæology was. The restoration of churches and cathedrals and the preservation of castles and other places of historical interest ought to be a matter of the greatest possible interest to the three great Masonic bodies we have named; and Freemasons at large, if they are worthy of their descent, and believe at all in the traditions of the Order, should surely show as keen a delight in these records of the past—these monuments of history—as do the outer world, who are not Masons. But do they? That is the question.

THIRD MINUTE BOOK.

THE third Minute Book of this old Lodge commences with a list of the members in 1786-7, and the account of their quarterly subscriptions, from which it would appear that they were all free from arrears with only one single exception, and that brother only owed for one quarter. I rather fancy there are a great many Lodges now-a-days would be glad to report so satisfactory a state of their financial condition. It may perhaps be of interest, at all events to the Freemasons in the Province of Suffolk, to give the names of the brethren who were members at this time. There were thirty-one in all, but one, Bro. Dagueville, I think the name is, appears to have resigned; and their names appear in the following order:—

John Spooner, Robert Manning, William Lane, senr., who is called throughout the records, the Operative Mason; Samuel Ribban, Robert Tovell, John Blomfield, James Woolward, John Humphrey, Thomas Askew, Benjamin Huggins, Joseph Scholding, Joseph Dobnam, William Lane, junr., Thomas Smith, innholder, Robert Turner, Robert Coles, Robert Cole, Robert Worth, John Ripshaw, John Gooding, William Morris, Thomas Smith, William P. Johnstone, Hugh Dyer, Richard Smith, Benjamin Dikes, William Marmall, Richard Lewis, Philip Hunt, Thomas Hinsby, William Churchman. In the list of members for the following year I find the name of William Middleton, Esq. No doubt this is the gentleman mentioned in my last paper as one of the candidates for the Prov. Grand Mastership of Suffolk. * Bro. Middleton's name with the affix carefully given, appears in 1789, and 1790, and 1791, as still belonging to the Lodge. And in the last-named year occur the names of James Devereux, C. Metralcourt, George Marven, and George Jermyn, all well-sounding names, but who the owners were I am not now able to ascertain.

Under date December 27th, 1786, St. John's Day, I find the

---

* He afterwards became Prov. G.M. as will be seen further on.

following minute: "Last Lodge night a motion being made by *several* brethren" (a new idea by the way), "and it was unanimously agreed to, that every member of this Lodge being absent from dinner on either of ye Festivals of St. John, to forfeit one shilling to ye fund of this Lodge," from which it would appear that at this time both Festivals were kept.

The Summer Festival, now known as the Feast of Roses, is evidently the outcome of this old custom, though it is not now held on the Saint's day. Neither is the Winter Festival kept on the 27th December; but whenever the Lodge happens to meet during that month, and the W.M. Elect is installed; and it is worthy of consideration whether a return to the old custom of a century ago is not desirable, and the Lodge might attend divine worship, as it did sometimes then, and celebrate the Festivals afterwards.

Amongst the other officers at this time I note a Senior and Junior Steward, and I think it best to call attention to this fact, for those officers are not now appointed in this Lodge I believe, nor in many others, which I think is a great mistake; their duties are to look after the brethren at refreshment, under the guidance of the M.C., and they should see that the banquet is properly served, that the waiters do their duty, and the guests paid due attention to. In the *Freemason's Manual*, an American work of some reputation, amongst other duties attached to their office, the Deacons are required to examine and *welcome* visiting brethren, and the Stewards are to provide refreshments and make a regular report of the expense to the Treasurer, also to see that the regalia of the Lodge are in good order and always ready for use. On appointment to office, the following is the address made to them by the Installating Master in America:

"Brothers,—You are appointed Stewards to this Lodge. The duties of your office are to assist in the collection of dues and

subscriptions; to keep an account of the Lodge expenses; to see
that the tables are properly furnished at refreshment, and that
every Brother is suitably provided for; and generally to assist the
Deacons and other Officers in performing their duties. Your
regular and early attendance will afford the best proof of your
zeal and attachment to the Lodge." From this it is apparent
that the office is by no means considered unimportant, and the
appointment of junior members to fulfil its functions will only
the better prepare them for other and more onerous duties.

On February 11th, 1787, a Lodge was convened at the "Sun"
in order to join in procession to attend the funeral of Bro. Fenton, a member of the Perfect Friendship Lodge. The following
Lodge night a pedestal, cushion, and stool were ordered for the
use of this Lodge, and they were accordingly provided at a cost
of £2 13s. 11d. by the meeting of the Lodge held in May, when
also a motion was made that a small subscription should be made
towards the expense of the burial of Bro. Thomas Colman, who
was unfortunately drowned—which was done. One is always
glad to come across these little evidences of the benevolent
character of our Order. Mere names are nothing, and one can
get but little idea of the status of the Lodge unless one knows
the social standing of its members.

One night I find a brandy merchant proposed, on another an
exciseman is admitted, and he soon after proposes another officer
of that much maligned body. At the June meeting, 1788, Bro.
William Middleton, Esq., was proposed by Bro. Ribbans as a
member of this Lodge, and his admission money, ten shillings,
was paid into the hands of the Treasurer. Bro. Middleton's attendance at the Lodge has been before noted.

In February, 1789, William Wade, Clerk to the Collector of
Excise, was proposed, and was admitted in March.

I am glad to notice a pencil note "free" against the names of visiting Brothers about this date, 1789. Mr. Thomas Wright, carpenter, of Copdock, Suffolk, was proposed at the meeting in December, which shows how various were the callings of the members of the Lodge at this time: I very much doubt whether a carpenter would have much chance of admission now. On the 2nd March, 1790, I find Bro. Russell, of the Philanthropic Lodge, Long Melford, Suffolk, a visitor of the Lodge. This Lodge is not now in existence, at all events it is not in the *Cosmopolitan Calendar*. The following Lodge night a visiting Brother from St. John's Lodge was present, but which of the St. John's I do not know.

Amongst the members present on the 5th October, 1790, we find the name of William Middleton, Esq., Prov. G.M. for the county, but there is no record as to when or where he was installed except the note below. It is a curious fact that the present justly-esteemed and very popular Prov. G.M., Lord Waveney, is also a member of this Lodge.

The next Lodge night, the 2nd November, the following minute occurs: "It was this evening proposed, and unanimously agreed, that a Lodge be convened for all the members of the Lodge that choose *to pass the chair;* and those absent, to be summoned for that purpose on Wednesday, the 3rd inst.; and it is further unanimously agreed that the tickets of admission on the day of Installation (sic) of Bro. Middleton shall be ten shillings and sixpence each." Accordingly on the following night I find that no less than twelve brethren passed the chair. Probably this was done to qualify them to attend the Installation of Bro. Middleton, as only W.M.'s, P.M.'s, and actual Wardens have a vote and seat in P.G.L. Allusion has before been made to this custom of giving brethren the rank of P.M., who never were Installed Masters, and there is therefore now no occasion to refer to a most objectionable practice, now happily obsolete.

At a meeting held December 7th, amongst the disbursements, I notice one that would strike our London brethren, "Paid to a Blue-coat Boy, one shilling." The Blue-coat Boy alluded to, however, was not one from the famous Christ's Hospital in London, but the little old building known as Christ's Hospital, at Ipswich, founded, I believe, in the reign of Queen Elizabeth. But why the boy got one shilling, and what he had to do with the Freemasons, I cannot tell. On St. John's Day of this year, a watchmaker, stationer, " gent," and upholsterer (sic) were proposed for initiation, and in the following March I find a wheelwright initiated.

The provincial clothing, I fancy, must have been a very different sort of thing to what it is now, when a full suit costs six or eight guineas, especially if got up in Bro. Kenning's best style. Under date April 5, 1791, I find—

" To two Provincial Aprons, three shillings and sixpence; each, seven shillings." I very much doubt whether a Prov. Gr. Officer could be found now who would condescend to wear a three shilling-and-sixpenny apron. On the 16th March, 1791, a general Lodge was convened at the " White Lion," St. Mary, Stoke, Ipswich, " to attend to ye funeral duties of Bro. T. Askew, in the churchyard of St. Mary, Stoke." Twenty brethren were present from the British Union, twelve from the Perfect Friendship Lodge, and five visitors. On the 30th of the same month I find that a general Lodge was held at the " Golden Lion," to attend the funeral duties of Bro. P. Hunt, who was also buried at St. Mary, Stoke, Ipswich. Eighteen members of the British Union were present, thirteen of the Perfect Friendship, and seven visitors.

In the Ancient and Accepted Rite abroad, what are called Funeral or Sorrow Lodges are always held, and in that valuable work, the *Monitor of the Ancient and Accepted Rite*, by Bro. E.

T. Carson 32°, we find an account of the grade in which these ceremonies are performed.

The degree is called Perfect Master, the 5th grade of the A. and A. Rite, and the second of the Ineffable series. Bro. Carson says: " This grade was originally established as a grateful tribute of respect to the memory of a departed worthy brother." Its ritual and lectures furnish many interesting details of the mode of his interment, and the honours paid to his memory. The ceremonies are gloomy and funereal, and well calculated to fill the mind with solemn thoughts. In this grade are held the Lodge of Sorrow, and are performed the funeral ceremonies of any brother of the sublime degree. The Lodge is hung with green tapestry on eight white columns, four in each side, at equal distances. It is illuminated by sixteen lights, four in each cardinal point. *

In Scotland, as well as in America, Sorrow Lodges are frequently held. In this country, however, we rarely or never read of such a thing in the *Freemason*, not even in the A. and A. Rite, which seems curious. The reason is probably because so few Masons are buried as Masons. In the United States, a great parade is made of Masonry; not so, however, in England. Except under very extraordinary circumstances, such as the Installation of the Prince of Wales, or the annual meeting of the Prov. Grand Lodge, in our various Provinces—the Masons in England rarely appear in public at all, and as the Constitutions only allow of a Masonic Funeral at the express desire of the deceased brother made (publicly, I believe) before his death, of course the occasions are few and far between, when Sorrow Lodge could appropriately be held, except by brethren of the high degrees, who are few in number, not more, I suppose, than a twentieth part of the Craft.

---

* The French say sixty-four, sixteen in each corner of the Lodge.

To return, however, to the Minutes of the British Union Lodge, I find an interesting one under date May 3rd, 1791 :

"This evening a motion was made by W.S.W., in full Lodge assembled, to send to the Royal Cumberland or Freemason's School ye sum of £1 1s.; and £1 1s. towards ye expenditure of the new Regalia, which is now fitting out at ye Grand Lodge, in honour of ye Prince of Wales, Grand Master of England. Ye above was seconded by ye R.W.M. and J.W., and unanimously agreed to by ye brethren present."

At the Lodge meeting, August 2nd, 1791, the Lodge was visited by Bro. Bazil Hown, or Heron, D.P.G.M., who appears to have been accompanied by Bros. J. R. Willett, P.G., Treasurer, and J. Thompson, M.D., P.G.S.W.; the P.G.M. Bro. Middleton was also present. If all Prov. Grand Masters make it a point of visiting every Lodge in their province, where it is a small one, once a year, and, where the province is large, as in E. and W. Lancashire, once in every two or three years, it would tend to uniformity of working—would bring them face to face with the real working Masons, and not merely the ornamental ones, and the result would be, a better selection of Provincial Grand Officers than is now often made—the doing away of many abuses that now exist, and it would prevent much of that heart-burning and petty jealousy, which unhappily have an existence even amongst Masons. It often happens, however, that the Prov. G.M. is a nobleman, whose political or other public duties prevent his paying that attention to the duties of his high office which his station demands. In such cases he should appoint as his deputy an energetic brother, of good social standing—a long purse and much leisure. Such men, and they are to be found, I am persuaded, in every province, might worthily fulfil the duties delegated to them, to the advancement of Masonry in general, and their own provinces in particular.

In September, 1791, it was found that the present expenditure was greater than the finances would allow, and the quarterly subscription was accordingly raised from four shillings to seven shillings and sixpence, a rather large increase. Two brethren resigned in consequence, but the great majority of the brethren appear to have been in favour of the change.

James Norford, a visiting Brother from the Royal Edwin Lodge, Bury St. Edmunds, was present at the December meeting. This Lodge, like the rest mentioned before, appears to have gone the way of all flesh; but when it became extinct I do not know.

So ends the third volume of the Old Minutes. The books are in bad condition, pages are cut out, and scarcely a leaf is whole. The Minutes are put in in the baldest possible way; but still I think have a little to interest the brethren of the mystic tie as to what occurred in our lodges, and what manner of men composed them, from the middle to the end of the eighteenth century.

NOTICE.

A Second Series of "TALES, POEMS, AND MASONIC PAPERS, BY EMRA HOLMES," uniform in size and price (2/6) with the present, is now preparing for publication, by special request, the profits to be devoted to the same good object. Subscribers' names to be sent to Tweddell and Sons, Stokesley, from whom alone copies can be obtained.

LIST OF SUBSCRIBERS.

Mr. John Abson, Rotherham
" John Allen, junr., Boston
" A. G. Anderson, Glasgow
" H. H. Andrew, Sheffield
William Andrews, Esq., F.R.H.S., Hull
Professor Ansted, Melton, Woodbridge
John Reed Appleton, Esq., F.S.A., Durham
Mr. S. Armstrong, Hartlepool
" Robert Arnison, Sheffield
" W. Ashworth, Rochdale
Wilfred Badger, Esq., Rotherham
Rev. A. A. Bagshawe, Wormhill Vicarage, Buxton
Mr. George Balmford, York
C. J. Banister, Esq., Summerhill House, Bradford
Mr. Frederick Barber, Sheffield
" John Barber, Mirfield
" William Barbour, Glasgow
" R. T. Barras, Sheffield
R. B. Barton, Esq., LL.D., J.P., Barrister-at-Law, Stour Lodge, Bradfield (four copies).
Mr. J. B. Bates, Newcastle-on-Tyne
H. H. Bedford, Esq., Birley House, Wadsley Bridge
John P. Bell, Esq., M.D., Waverley House, Hull
Mr. F. W. Bell, Liverpool
" Stephen Binckes, Horncastle
" H. J. Bingham, Rotherham
Joseph Binney, Esq., Sheffield
Mr. Joseph Bland, Derby
" Richard Boggett, Paragon Hotel, Hull (four copies).
" Isaac Booth, Halifax
The Hon. R. F. Bower, Keokuk, Iowa, U.S.A.
Mr. Henry Bowes, Stokesley
Rev. Dr. E. Brette, Christ's Hospital, London
Mr. James Brimmer, Dundee
The Most Noble the Marquis of Bristol (two copies).
Mr. W. H. Brittain, Sheffield

Mr. C. P. Brockbank, Bolton
„ Joseph Bromley, Sheffield
Miss Brook, Woodbridge
Mr. James Brown, Doncaster
„ H. M. Cairson, Ipswich
„ J. W. Carmichael, Dublin
The Right Hon. the Earl of Carnarvon, P.C.
Joseph Chapman, Esq., Grimsby (six copies).
Mr. John Clark, Sheffield
„ Walter Clark, do.
„ Thos. Clarke, do.
„ M. G. Collingwood, Middlesbrough
Miss E. Colling, Hurworth
D. Colquhoun, Esq., Dublin (two copies).
Sir Patrick Colquhoun, Q.C., London
Mr. John Constable, London
„ Joseph Cook, Stockton-on-Tees
„ James Cooke, Glasgow
„ D. Cooper, Dublin (two copies).
„ Thomas Cooper, York
The Right Hon. Lord Cottesloe (two copies).
Mr. John Dale, Middlesbrough
„ John Dallerger, Woodbridge
W. R. Dalton, Esq., Dep. Inspector Gen. R.N., Dovercourt.
William Danby, Esq, Elmfield House, Exeter.
Mr. J. E. Darling, Sheffield
„ William Deanham, Scarborough
Joseph Dodds, Esq., M.P., Stockton-on-Tees (two copies).
Mr. J. G. Douglas, Hartlepool
„ William Douglas, Dundee
G. W. Douglas, Esq., Ipswich
Sir Francis Doyle, Professor of Poetry, Oxford
Mr. Ensor Drury, Sheffield
„ H. A. Dubois, London
„ J. Dunlop, Harwich
„ Henry Ecroyd, Oughtibridge
Lieut.-Col. Sir Henry Edwards, Bart., J.P., D.L. (four copies).
Lady Edwards, Pye Nest, near Halifax (four copies).
T. K. Elkington, Esq., Ipswich
Mr. J. G. Elliott, Sheffield
S. B. Ellis, Esq., Sheffield
Rev. John Emra, Biddleston Rectory (three copies).
Mr. C. H. Erentz, Dundee
C. H. Ewing, Esq., Dublin (twelve copies).
Mr. Alfred Farnworth, Glasgow
„ John Fawcett, Rotherham
„ James Ferguson, Boston

William Few, Esq., M.R.C.S., Ramsey (two copies).
H. Fisher, Esq., Woodbridge
S. Ll. Foster, Esq., London (two copies).
Mr. Donald Fraser, Glasgow.
 ,, George Freeman, Woodbridge
Alfred Fuller, Esq., Ramsey (four copies).
Mr. B. Gall, Woodbridge
 ,, H. J. Garnett, Sheffield
 ,, S. S. Gayley, Liverpool
 ,, Robert Gildea, Dundee
 ,, J. S. Gissing, Woodbridge
 ,, A. E. J. Givero, Glasgow
 ,, John Golden, Plantation House, Ramsey
F. Goulburn, Esq., C.B., Chairman of the Board of Customs, London (four copies).
Mr. J. W. Gould, Hull
 ,, E. B. Grabham, London
 ,, T. G. Graham, Glasgow
 ,, Robert Grainger, Skibbereen (four copies).
Dr. Greene, Ennis, Co. Clare
Mrs. Green,   do.
Miss Alice Green   do.
F. Griffiths, Esq., M.D., Carlton House, Sharrow.
G. A. Grimwood, Esq., Shern Hall, Walthamstow (two copies).
W. A. Guiston, Esq., M.D., Manor House, Ipswich
Mr. G. W. Haggard, Rotherham.
Rev. A. W. Hamilton, M.A., Mus. Bac., Vicar of Stanton, Rowton Hall, Derbyshire.
J. H. Handyside, Esq., Stokesley
John Harrison, Esq., Haughley, Suffolk
J. B. Hart, Esq., Woodbridge
Mr. Charles Harvey, Rotherham
 ,, Simeon Hayes, Sheffield.
J. J. Head, Esq, Deal
The Right Hon. Lord Henniker (two copies).
J. L. Henry, Esq., Peterhead
Lord John W. N. Hervey (two copies).
John Hervey, Esq., Grand Sec., Freemasons' Hall, London (two copies).
Henry Hewith, Esq., Woodbridge
Mr. Charles Hill, Sheffield
 ,, A. P. Hirst, Rotherham.
 ,, John Hoggan, Glasgow
H. M. Holmes, Esq., Mason, Mason County, Texas (two copies).
W. H. Holmes, Esq., Stockton-on-Tees
Henry Horncastle, Esq., Whitmoor House, Ollerton (two copies).
Rev. W. Horpur, St. Mary's Vicarage, Ramsey

W. J. Hughan, Esq., Truro
The Library of the Grand Lodge of Iowa, U.S.A.
Capt. Irvin, Bristol
Mr. H. W. Jackman, Glasgow
 ,, William Jervis, Sheffield.
 ,, Thomas Jones, Ruperra House, Brecon
 ,, John Jordison, Middlesbrough
 ,, R. M. Kelly, Glasgow
 ,, Samuel Kelly, London
 ,, W. H. Kidd, Hull
 ,, John Kirkpatrick, Dundee
 ,, James Knight,   do.
 ,, A. E. Law, Sheffield
E. C. Lawson, Esq., Newcastle-on-Tyne (two copies).
F. Leech, Esq., Eccles (two copies).
The Right Hon. Lord Leigh
The Right Hon. the Earl of Limerick
R. W. Little, Esq., Sec. to the Royal Masonic Institution for
    Girls, London.
Mr. H. W. Lofthouse, Sheffield
 ,, Frederick Long, Stowmarket
Peter de Lande Long, Esq., London
J. Mackenzie, Esq., Leith (two copies).
Mr. Hugh Mac Innes, Glasgow
 ,, F. M. Macqueen, Woodbridge
 ,, H. C. Manners, West Hartlepool
Rev. C. J. Martyn, Rector of Melford (two copies).
Mr. William Mason, Middlesbrough
 ,, Henry Matthews, Sheffield
Mrs. C. Mawdesley, Great Whyte, Ramsey
 ,, T. S. Mawdesley, Ramsey (two copies).
Mr. William Mellersh, Liverpool (two copies).
 ,, James Merrick, Bristol
C. E. Meyer, Esq., Philadelphia, U.S.A. (two copies).
Mr. H. H. Meyer, West Hartlepool.
Middlesbrough Police Library
L. R. Mitchell, Glasgow
John B. Monckton, Esq., Town Clerk of London
George Moore, Esq., M.D., Hartlepool (six copies).
J. D. Moore, Esq., M.D., F.Z.S., Lancaster (two copies).
John Moore, Esq., Orient of Ottawa, Canada (two copies).
W. A. Moore, Esq., M.R.C.S., Woodbridge.
J. T. Muriel, Esq., M.R.C.S., Hadleigh
Mr. J. G. Needham, Rotherham
The Right Hon. the Earl Nelson (four copies).
Mr. Bernard Nicholson, Sheffield
J. H. Nielson, Esq., Dublin

Mr. Herbert Nixon, M.R.C.V.S., Sheffield
,, T. H. North, Middlesbrough (two copies).
Henry Oldland, Esq., Avon Grove, Stoke Bishop, Bristol
Mr. A. Oldroyd, Leyton
Richard Ord, Esq., J.P., Stockton-on-Tees
Mr. Robert Owen, Bangor
Elgar Pagden, Esq., Sunderland
Mr. J. W. Palmer, Boston
,, Robert Patrick, Glasgow
,, H. W. Pawson, Sheffield
The Library of the Grand Lodge of Philadelphia, Pennsylvania, U.S.A.
C. H. Perrot, Esq., Rotherham.
Miss Isabella Philips, Penmoyle, Chepstow (two copies).
J. N. Pickering, Esq., Sheffield
Mr. Thomas Playford, Orford
,, William Pratt, Ipswich
W. F. Pratt, Esq., Stokesley.
Mr. Henry Preston, Hull
John Prior, Esq., Ipswich (two copies).
G. G. Pye, Esq., Colchester
Mr. I. T. Pytches, Melton, Woodbridge
H. Quirheirth, Esq., Fern Brae, West Newport, Fife
Mr. J. R. R. Rayner, Glasgow
,, A. W. Read, Boston
,, L. C. Read, King's Lynn
,, J. E. Reaney, Sheffield
,, J. C. Redgrave, Rotherham
,, Samuel Rees, Harwich
Benjamin Richardson, Esq., M.R.C.S., Glaisdale
Mr. John Robson, Middlesbrough
,, L. W. Roddewig, Sheffield
W. R. Ross, Esq., Glasgow
Mr. Benjamin Saville, Rotherham
,, Alfred Scargill, Sheffield
Commander Charles Scott. R.N., J.P., Strathray, Omagh, Ireland
Mr. Andrew Scott, Glasgow
Henry Seebohm, Esq., F.Z.S., Rutledge, Sheffield
,, Sergeant, Ramsey (two copies).
Mr. W. Sharpe, Ingleby Junction
Bentley Shaw, Esq., J.P., Woodfield House, Huddersfield (two copies).
The Sheffield Masonic Library
Mr. J. H. Shields, Glasgow
The Right Hon. Lord Skelmersdale (two copies).
Mr. A. M. Smith, Glasgow
,, R. S. Smyth,   do.

Mr. C. S. Spalding, Glasgow
„ Frederick Spalding, Woodbridge
„ J. G. Speed, Ulverston
„ Joseph Spencer, Sheffield
The Right Hon. the Earl Stanhope (six copies).
John Sutcliffe, Esq., Grimsby (six copies).
Mr. H. Sutcliffe, Manchester
„ Jack Sutcliffe, Grimsby
„ D. Sydenham, Bournemouth (twelve copies).
„ H. L. Tacon, Rotherham
J. E. Taylor, Esq., F.G.S., Ph. D., F.L.S., Ipswich
J. Terry, Esq., Sec. to the Royal Masonic Benevolent Institution,
    London (two copies).
W. R. Thomas, Esq., M.D., Sheffield
Mr. James Thomson, Shawdon
„ E. C. Tidd, London
Rev. A. Tighe-Gregory, Vicar of Bawdsey
Mr. F. M. Tindall, Sheffield (two copies).
„ C. C. Tourner, Grundisburgh
Nathaniel Tracy, Esq., Ipswich
Mr. John Trenholm, Stockton-on-Tees
F. Tricket, Esq., Brincliffe, Sheffield (two copies).
Rev. Canon Tristram, LL.D., F.R.S., Durham
Edward Turnbull, Esq., West Hartlepool (two copies).
Mr. Thomas Tweddell, Stokesley
„ John Unwin, junr., Sheffield
„ T. H. Vernon, Sheffield
W. S. Wade, Esq., Wakefield
Mr. John Waller, Whitby
Mrs. Wasbrough, Willsbridge, Bristol
„ Charles Wasbrough,   do.   (six copies).
A. A. Watts, Esq., Ipswich
Mr. John Watts, Manchester
The Right Hon. Lord Waveney
F. Webber, Esq., Louisville, Kentucky, U.S.A.
Mr. George Weir, Glasgow
William White, Esq., Sheffield
Mr. T. B. Whytehead, York
William Wilcox, Esq., Scarborough (six copies.)
Rev. W. Wilkinson, De Crespigny House, Aldeburgh, Suffolk
    (two copies).
Mr. E. G. Willes, Aldeburgh, Suffolk
„ T. D. Wing, Hull.
Rev. A. F. A. Woodford, M.A., London (four copies).
Mr. J. B. Wostinholm, Sheffield
„ J. H. Wragg, Rotherham
J. R. Wright, Esq., Sheffield

L. H. Wyatt, Esq., H.M.S. *Favorite*, Frith of Forth.
John Yarker, Esq., Manchester.

NOTICE.

Those subscribers who have not already paid for their copies are kindly requested to remit the amount to Tweddell and Sons, Stokesley, Yorkshire, on receipt of the present work, and to state if they wish their names to be retained as subscribers to the Second Series. Thanks are gratefully tendered to them for their liberal patronage; also to those friends who have disinterestedly assisted to procure subscribers, especially to Mr. W. J. Hughan, of Truro, Mr. Jackman and Mr. Moxon, of Glasgow, Mr. J. Watson, Boston, and, above all, to Mr. S. B. Ellis, of Sheffield, who procured subscriptions for no less than 102 copies.

A new edition of the popular Serenade, *A Lover's Watch*, written and composed by EMRA HOLMES, arranged by CHRISTOPHER HOGGETT, and commended by the metropolitan and provincial press, is now preparing for publication, price 1s. 3d., the profits to be devoted to the same object as those of the present volume. Subscribers' names thankfully received by the Publishers as above.

PUBLICATIONS NOW ON SALE BY TWEDDELL AND SONS, STOKESLEY.

In one beautifully printed volume of 286 pages, crown 8vo., cloth, gilt lettered, reduced from 5s. to 3s. 6d., or free by bookpost 4s., the entire profits to be devoted to the same benevolent object as those of the present volume,

The Story of Count Ulaski; Aurelia, or the Gifted, and other original Poems, with Translations.

By ETA MAWR.

COMMENDATIONS OF ETA MAWR'S POEMS.

"An eloquent volume. . . . I find much to admire in 'Count Ulaski' and 'Aurelia,' especially the latter, and the Translations appear to me composed with rare ease and felicity. They introduce me to many poems with which I was before unacquainted."—Lord Lytton.

"A very pleasing and delightful volume . . . The charm of metre goes a good way with me, and I like to pause and linger over flowing and graceful verse, and that yours most assuredly is. . . . But to return to those two tales, 'Ulaski' and 'Aurelia,' they are full of interest, the one of active, the other of sedentary interest, or, as the Germans would distinguish them, of objective and subjective interest. . . . I have read the minor poems also with a great deal of enjoyment. The 'Sonnet to Handel' struck me as particularly good. 'The Stocking Knitter' is a gem."—Sir J. Herschel.

"I like your 'Aurelia' exceedingly, and your 'Golden Mean.' Your verses are loaded with thought."—Rev. George Gilfillan.

"In the volume before us there are a thousand beauties. . . . We really think that no fruits of the modern muse contain finer passages, or show deeper knowledge of the human heart than 'Ulaski' and 'Aurelia.' . . . The minor poems, both original and from the German, have genuine force and sweetness. . . . The 'Poet of Coila' has never been greeted with a more just, a more eloquent, or a more charming eulogium. . . . The noblest efforts of Burns's genius, and the finest qualities in those efforts, are referred to with equal warmth of admiration, and soundness of critical judgment. The tributes entitled 'Gibsoniana' are warm, genial, graceful, eloquent, and well deserved, for undoubtedly Gibson stands on the highest roll of British sculptors."—Durham Advertiser.

"Her translations of German poetry are excellent and well selected, and, taking her book altogether, it is decidedly an honour to the head and heart of the authoress."—Illustrated Times.

"Here we have in a small compass a great deal of very good poetry. . . . The present volume fully sustains, and, we think, adds in no small degree to the reputation achieved by its predecessor."—W. T. Kime, Esq., Barrister-at-Law, J.P., Editor of "Albert the Good," &c.

"In reviving the memory of poor Poland you have struck most forcibly the chords of my heart, for from a very early age I have felt for its sufferings a sincere sympathy."—M. G. Solling, a German correspondent.

NORTH OF ENGLAND TRACTATES.

Under the above title, the Publishers purpose to print, from time to time, a collection of small Treatises, in prose and verse, relating to the North of England, offering them to the general public at the lowest possible prices which will clear the necessary expenses of publication. The following are now ready, at One Penny Each.

No. 1.—*Cleveland*, a Poem, in Blank Verse, by JOHN REED APPLETON, F.S.A.; with Tailpiece.

No. 2.—*Prince Oswy*, a Legend of Rosebury Topping, by the late JOHN WALKER ORD, F.G.S.L.

No. 3.—*The Trials and Troubles of a Tourist*, by JOHN REED APPLETON, F.R.S.N.A.; with Tailpieces by Bewick and Linton.

No. 4.—*Rhymes to Illustrate the North York Dialect*, by FLORENCE CLEVELAND.

No. 5.—*Yorkshire Worthies*, by JOHN RYLEY ROBINSON, LL.D., with Medallion of Capt. Cook.

No. 6.—*The Old, Old Woman of Elton*, a Ballad, by ETA MAWR; with Tailpiece by Linton.

No. 7.—*Cleveland Sonnets*, by GEORGE MARKHAM TWEDDELL.

No. 8.—*Halifax Gibbet and Gibbet Law*, by JOHN RYLEY ROBINSON, LL.D.; with illustrations.

No. 9.—*Howley Hall*, a Prose Sketch; and *Rosebury Topping*, a Blank Verse Poem, by JOHN RYLEY ROBINSON, LL.D.; with Tailpiece by Bewick.

No. 10.—*Sunnyside Gill*, a Blank Verse Poem, by GEORGE MARKHAM TWEDDELL, F.R.S.N.A., Copenhagen, &c.

No. 11.—*Cleveland Thoughts, or the Poetry of Toil*, a Blank Verse Poem, by ANGUS MACPHERSON, C.E.; with Tailpiece by Bewick.

No. 12.—*The Saxon Cross, Church, &c., at Dewsbury*, by JOHN RYLEY ROBINSON, LL.D.; with four fine Illustrations, and a Linton Tailpiece.

No. 13.—*Awd Gab, o' Steers; How he Tried to Sweetheart Betty Moss: a Trew Tedle*, related in the North York Dialect, by FLORENCE CLEVELAND; with a Glossary.

No. 14.—*The Chestnut Knight, or Origin of English Album Making*, a Ballad, by the late MAURICE H. DALE; with a Portrait of Lambert Russell, and a Tailpiece by Bewick.

No. 15.—*In Memoriam. On the Death of Mark Philips, Esq.*, a Blank Verse Poem, by GEORGE MARKHAM TWEDDELL.

No. 16.—*The Baron of Greystoke*, a Legendary Ballad; by the REV. JAMES HOLME, B.A., late Vicar of Kirkleatham.

No. 17.—*A Voice from Flood and Fell*, by the late J. G. GRANT.

Complete in one volume of 100 pages, fscp. 8vo., printed on good paper, bound in blue cloth, gilt lettered, price 1s. 6d., or strongly bound and richly ornamented, 2s. 6d.; by bookpost 2d. extra.

RHYMES AND SKETCHES TO ILLUSTRATE THE CLEVELAND DIALECT,

By Mrs. G. M. Tweddell (*Florence Cleveland*).

COMMENDATIONS.

From His Grace the Archbishop of York.—"An interesting volume of *Sketches*. It has, besides its poetical interest, a certain philological interest too. I am very glad to possess it."

From Robert Henry Allan, Esq., F.S.A., J.P., D.L., &c., of Blackwell Hall.—"My dear Mr. Tweddell, I have received three copies of Mrs. Tweddell's elegant and clever volume. The *Sketches* are very characteristic and most amusing; and the Glossary is as essentially necessary as it is valuable. . . Will you kindly send me twenty-seven extra bound copies (2/6 each), which, with the three copies just received, will make up the thirty copies subscribed for by Mrs. Allan and myself, for which I beg leave to enclose a cheque on Messrs. Backhouse and Co. for £5, and which you will be so obliging as to hand to Mrs. Tweddell with our united compliments."

From the Rev. T. P. Williamson (formerly of Gisbrough) Vicar of Little Brickhill, Bucks., Author of *If Either—Which*, &c.—"Alluding to your Preface, I may say, that it is a happy thing that no other person *was* writing in the Cleveland Dialect at this time; for I am certain no other person could have produced so delightful a little book as yours. It is not only the 'Cleveland Dialect' very happily rendered, but the whole (whether poetry or prose) hits off the Cleveland *character* of a former day in a way that leaves nothing to be desired."

From the Rev. James Holme, B.A., late Vicar of Kirkleatham, Author of *Leisure Musings and Devotional Meditations, Mount Grace Abbey, and other Poems*.—"I have long intended to write and thank you for the beautiful little volume of your excellent rustic poems."

From Mr. J. H. Eccles, of Leeds, Author of *Yorkshire Songs*, &c.—"I like both Poems and Sketches very much, and think they are a credit both to your *head* and *heart*. . . . Believe me to be your sincere wisher, that the work may have the popularity it deserves, and dear old Cleveland furnish you with themes for many poems and sketches of such naturalness and beauty."

From William Danby, Esq., of Elmfield House, Exeter (formerly of Gisbrough), Author of *Poems*, &c.—"I received Mrs. Tweddell's book on Saturday night, and enclose stamps. It was, as Uriah Heap says, 'like the ringing of old bellses' to hear, as it were, through the void of time, the sound of the robust vernacular of my native district. . . I have already had great pleasure in reading several of the pieces, and am looking forward to the opportunity of making myself acquainted with the rest. . I can only hope that many 'Bobs' may be induced to 'stop at yam' at nights, and read Mrs. Tweddell's sound moral lessons, and occasional pathetic utterances, to their families. The railways, and the vast introduction of an abnormal population, consequent on the development of the iron trade, must have gone far to banish much of the old Dialect, and induce many natives to attempt a more cosmopolitan mode of speech; and therefore we should be the more obliged to Mrs. Tweddell for her endeavour that it should not be wholly forgotten. She has done for the North Riding what Hughes has done for Wiltshire, Barnes for Dorsetshire, 'Nathan Hogg' for Devonshire, Tregellas for Cornwall, and other writers for other counties."

From Eta Mawr, Authoress of *Far and Near*, *The Story of Count Ulaski, Aurelia, and other Poems*, &c.—" Accept my best thanks, my dear 'Florence Cleveland,' for the elegantly bound copy of your *Rhymes and Sketches to illustrate the Cleveland Dialect*, whose contents I had already devoured in their humbler garb, with much admiration of the skill and talent, the wit and humour, of the clever authoress, and the excellent moral tone everywhere, but unobtrusively, pervading it. . . I hope your little book will have customers among the class who speak its language, and that both wives and husbands will benefit by such moral lessons as are conveyed in 'Come, stop at yam te neet, Bob,' &c. Of the prose *Sketches* my favourite is the inimitable 'Betty Moth,' but they are all very good in their way."

From Mr. W. M. Egglestone, Author of *Weardale Forest*.— " When I came home last night, Mrs. Tweddell's Cleveland Sketches was on my table. I glanced through the work, and read 'Stowslay Cattle Show,' which pleased me very much. With some trifling exceptions, the Cleveland Dialect is very much like that of Weardale. How Bill and Polly *liked* each other, and how they bungled about expressing their love, their sweet-hearting at the gate, &c., is very much like the style how a Weardale lad and lass, twenty years ago, would have done. The sketch of ' Polly Rivers's Trip te Stowslay Cattle Show' reads as if it had been taken down in shorthand from the lips of the veritable Polly, it is so life-like and interesting."

From the late Alexander Craig Gibson, Esq., F.S.A., with a presentation copy of his admirable work on *The Folk-Speech of Cumberland and some Districts adjacent*.—" With the Author's kind regards to Mrs. G. M. Tweddell, in whom he is gratified to have discovered a congenial taste."

From Mr. William Andrews, F.R.H.S., Author of *The History of the Dunmore Flitch*, &c.—" I am very much pleased with Mrs. Tweddell's volume, and so are all those who have seen it. Though I like all the pieces, the poem on 'T' Awd Cleveland Customs' delights me most."

From Mr. F. K. Robinson, Author of *A Glossary of Yorkshire Words and Phrases, collected in Whitby and the Neighbourhood; Whitby: its Abbey, and the principal parts of the Neighbourhood,* &c.—" Florence Cleveland is very happy in her North Yorkshire productions. She has both an eye and an ear for its picturesque and expressive Dialect."

From Louis H. Phillips, Esq., Barrister-at-Law.—" I have to thank you very much for Mrs. Tweddell's most interesting book, which I have just finished reading. It is really a refreshing and agreeable contribution to the local literature of the day; and you may take my compliment (such as it is worth) as the more sincere in that I am no admirer of *local*, by which I mean *dialect*, verses or sketches as a rule. I admit their *value* in their place, for special and antiquarian purposes; but as Johnson said about wines, 'they are not for me.' If the book had not been your wife's, probably I should not have looked at it. As it is, I own myself rewarded."

From Mrs. Macquoid, Authoress of *Forgotten by the World, Hester Kirton, By the Sea, Doris Barugh,* &c.—" Please thank Mrs. Tweddell for the pleasure her verses have given us. Some of them are very pretty."

The above are selected from scores of others, from all classes of persons. The following London and provincial publications have also commended the work, viz.—The Archæologist, the Barnsley Chronicle, the Barnsley Times, the Bradford Chronicle, the Chelsea Times, the City Press, the Criterion, the Derbyshire Courier, the Durham Advertiser, the Durham Chronicle, the Eastern Morning News, the Freemason, the Gisbrough Exchange, the Harrogate Gazette, the Hull News, the Hull Packet, Iron, the Knaresbro' Times, the Leamington Courier, the Leeds Mercury, Lloyd's Weekly London Newspaper, the Masonic Magazine, the Middlesbrough Exchange, the Middlesbrough News, the Middlesbrough and Stockton Gazette, the Middlesbrough Temperance Visitor, the Newcastle Daily Chronicle, the Northern Echo, the Otley News, the Pictorial World, the Sheffield Times and Iris, the South Durham Herald, the Sunderland Times, the Tadcaster Post, the Waikouaiti and Shag Valley Herald (Hawksbury, Province of Otago, New Zealand), the Wakefield Free Press, the Westminster Chronicle, the Wetherby News, the Whitby Gazette, the Whitby Times, the York Hera'd, the Yorkshire Gazette, the Yorkshire Post, and others.

THE GREAT AMERICAN MASONIC POEM.

Price 2d., or sent post free to any part of Great Britain or Ireland on receipt of five halfpenny postage stamps,

KING SOLOMON'S TEMPLE,

A MASONIC POEM,

BY BRO. AUGUSTINE J. H. DUGANNE,

OF NEW YORK CITY.

"Whether we consider its unusual length, the facility of its expression, the fervent glow of its imagery, its flowing versification, or that grand poetical *............* which bespeaks its author truly a poet, it may be re*...............*, and without a fault, as the finest Masonic poem in the *................*"—American Freemason.

"*................* owe a debt of gratitude to Bro. Tweddell for bringing *............* reach, in this exceedingly cheap and compendious form, the *............* of Masonic poetry. This beautiful production was written by *............* J. H. Duganne, of New York, a brother who, we rejoice to say, *............* and enjoys the confidence and esteem of his fellow-citizens *............* remembered by our readers, that our contributor, 'The *............* Sch*........*,' quoted three stanzas from this remarkable poem in the *............* of his 'Freemasonry in England,' in No. 60, and from *............* the brethren can imagine how exquisite and unique is the completed poem." —The Freemason.

"*............* poem cannot be otherwise than deeply interesting to every judicious reader, and *................* so to the members of the ancient Craft."—Redcar and Saltburn *......*

"One of the finest pieces of Speculative Masonry in the literature of any nation."—Middlesbrough Exchange.

"The metre of the poem is easy and flowing, and the language chaste and vigorous."—Middlesbrough News.

"The poem is a grand production, and worthy of the Craft, and of the United States masonically,—which is saying a great deal, as the Fraternity in the Eastern Hemisphere are at the front in all matters appertaining to the History, Ceremonies, or Regulations of our Institutions."—Bro. W. J. Hughan, P.M., P.S.G.D., P. Prov. G. Sec. for Cornwall, &c.

"The Fraternity have to thank Bro. Tweddell for his reproduction, in a cheap though neat form, of THE Masonic poem of the day—an allegorical piece, entitled 'King Solomon's Temple,' in which the symbolism of the Craft is introduced with a copiousness and oppositeness that stamps the work as 'a mighty Masonic Psalm' indeed, highly to be commended to the Brotherhood."—Bro. David Murray Lyon, P.M., Sec. to the Grand Lodge of *............* &c.

"*............* Tweddell (one of the firm being Bro. Geo. M. Tweddell, F.S.A., &c., *............* will be familiarly known to our readers as a very old contributor to these pages) have recently re-printed and issued this striking Masonic Poem in the shape of a neat pamphlet. Messrs. Tweddell deserve credit for the perception they have shown in selecting this admirable Masonic Poem for reproduction in this country. The beautiful allegory which pervades its flowing versification throughout, the happiness of its expression, and allusions, commend it to the study and perusal of every member of the Order.'—Freemason's Magazine.

₀ Where six or more copies are ordered, no charge will be **made** for Postage.

Reduced from 1s. 6d. to 1s., or post free to any part of Great Britain or Ireland on receipt of fourteen penny postage stamps,

With a Map of the District on both sides of Tees Bay, the second edition, revised by the Author, of

THE VISITOR'S HANDBOOK TO REDCAR
COATHAM, AND SALTBURN-BY-THE-SEA,

With Historical and Descriptive Accounts of Places of Interest in the Neighbourhood suitable for Rambles.

By GEORGE MARKHAM TWEDDELL.

"I have received so much pleasure from its perusal and guidance through the Saltburn locality, that I consider it cheap at even double its price."—John Reed Appleton, Esq., F.S.A.

"This little book, which has reached its second edition, will find a welcome place in the knapsack of every traveller visiting the delightful retreats upon which it dilates. It is full of interesting and valuable information, historical and descriptive, which is given in the familiar and easy style so desirable and proper in productions of this nature. The author has availed himself largely of authorities bearing upon the subjects before him, but his quotations are well chosen for their direct applicability, and are connected in a happy and judicious manner. The poetical illustrations, drawn from some of our best poets, tend to diversify the character of the work, and, being everywhere exceedingly appropriate, they are by no means the least interesting features in this useful and entertaining little handbook, which may be safely recommended to the notice of all who take an interest in the charming locality of which it treats."—Middlesbro' News.

"Visitors to Redcar wish to know something about the antecedents of the place, and Mr. Tweddell has thrown many pleasing and antiquarian researches together to make a useful book for their information. The adjacent villages and things of note are treated of, and the attention of visitors called to many interesting places and objects which are noted in the neighbourhood. Mr. Tweddell has done the public service in printing a second edition of his interesting little work, which will not fail to please and be useful to all who read it."—Stockton Herald.

"The writer of this little volume has for many years been well known as the author of several works of considerable literary merit, amongst which that of 'Shakspere, his Times and Contemporaries,' is undoubtedly his best, and occupies no mean rank in the voluminous literature relating to the 'myriad-minded bard of Avon.' The reputation Mr. Tweddell has earned for himself by the work just mentioned is fully sustained in the present publication. Being a native of a locality adjoining that which he describes, and possessing an immense fund of local, antiquarian, topographical, and historical information, combined with mental gifts of a very high order, he was well qualified for the task he undertook in the production of a handbook to Redcar and its vicinity. The work shows evidences of a very extensive research for facts relating to the places he describes, which he has used in a most judicious manner. His descriptions are full and accurate, and a vein of genuine humour runs through the work, relieving it of that dull and tedious air which is so characteristic of works of this class. In short, it does much credit to the taste, industry, and ability of its author. Every visitor to Redcar or the neighbourhood should provide himself with this handbook, and thus secure one of the best of guides and companions for his rambles."—Stockton Gazette and Middlesbrough Times.

TESTIMONIAL
TO
GEORGE MARKHAM TWEDDELL.

It has long been the wish of many of the friends and admirers of this well known Author and Public Speaker, to present him with some substantial Testimonial of esteem, for his life-long Labours for the Mental and Moral Elevation of the People. There has scarcely been a movement in the path of Progress which he has not aided, publicly and privately, by his tongue and pen, from his youth up to the present time; often at a great pecuniary loss to himself; so that many, who may have differed widely from him in opinion, have not hesitated to express their admiration of the enthusiastic and unflinching manner in which he has always devoted his abilities in striving to promote whatever appeared to him to be for the good of humanity, whether popular or otherwise. The present Testimonial will consist of a PURSE OF GOLD, to help him through heavy losses and family affliction, over which he has no control, and to aid him to complete those Literary Labours in which he is known to have been so long engaged; whilst to preserve an enduring record of its presentation, the names of all the Subscribers, whether of pounds or of pence, will be printed in book form, and copies deposited in all the principal public libraries, as well as distributed among the Subscribers. The Testimonial will not be of a Sectarian, Party, or even Local character; and Subscriptions for the same will be gladly received, and duly acknowledged, by

Wm. Andrews, F.R.H.S., No. 10, Colonial Street, Hull.
Charles Bell, Draper, 1, Sussex-street, Middlesbrough, and High-street, Redcar.
Isaac Binns, F.R.H.S., Borough Accountant, Batley.
R. Broadbridge, Minister of the Unsectarian Church, Wilnecote, near Tamworth.
A. J. Broadbridge, Overseer's Office, Middlesbrough.
J. Tom Burgess, F.S.A., Grassbrooke, Leamington.

W. H. Burnett, Editor of the *Daily Exchange*, Middlesbrough.
F. B. Cooke, Manager of the National Provincial Bank of England, Stokesley.
T. W. Craster, M.D., Linthorpe Road, Middlesbrough.
L. F. Crummey, M.R.C.S., Manor House, Great Ayton.
John Dixon, Merchant, Skelton, via Marske-by-the-Sea.
John Dunning, Ex-Mayor, Southfield Villas, Middlesbrough.
J. F. Elgee, Manager of Backhouse and Co's Bank, Middlesbro'.
Thomas B. Forster (Sec. to the " Wharton " Lodge, I.O. Oddfellows), 32, High-street, Skelton, Cleveland.
Joseph Gould, Printer, 24, South-street, Middlesbrough.
Spencer T. Hall, "The Sherwood Forester," Burnley.
Emra Holmes, Collector of Customs, Fowey, Cornwall.
George Kenning, Masonic Jeweller and Publisher, 198, Fleet-street, 1, 2, and 3, Little Britain, and 175, Aldersgate-street, London; 2, Monument Place, Liverpool; and 9, West Howard-street, Glasgow.
Samuel F. Longstaffe, F.R.H.S., Norton Green, Stockton-on-Tees.
John Macfarlane and Sons, Booksellers, Middlesbrough.
Wm. Mason, Berlin House, Newport Road, Middlesbrough.
David Normington, Watchmaker, Stokesley.
Rev. John Oxlee, Rector of Cowesby, via Thirsk.
Thomas Rawling (Sec. to Stokesley District I.O. Oddfellows), Stamp Office, Gisbrough.
Henry Roberts, 37, Rushford-street, Middlesbrough.
John Ryley Robinson, LL.D., Westgate, Dewsbury.
John Sutherst, Cleveland Ironworks, Gisbrough.
Fred. Wake (Sec. to Friendly Dividend Society), Carlton-in-Cleveland.
George Watson, J.P., Cleveland Villas, Middlesbrough.
Richard Watson, Manager of the Darlington District Joint Stock Bank, Stokesley.
Thomas Watson, Auctioneer, 4, Grange Road, Darlington.

Persons wishing to be added to the above List, are requested to send their names and addresses to

WILLIAM ANDREWS, F.R.H.S.,
Honorary Secretary.

No. 10, Colonial Street, Hull,
June, 1877.

www.ingramcontent.com/pod-product-compliance
Lightning Source LLC
Chambersburg PA
CBHW021836230426
43669CB00008B/988